This book is written to honor the memory of Pope John Paul II and Saint Faustina Kowalska, in gratitude for the tremendous legacy they have left us all. We also remember sister Leonella Agorbati, and Dr. Homa Darabi, whose untimely deaths remind us how fragile life under tyranny can be. We also recall with joyful thanks all the Holy men and women who have touched our individual lives, along with the lives of countless others they serve across the world. In reading this book may we realize just as Pope John Paul II taught us, the value of every human being, and learn to love and live together in peace and harmony.

The Last Wish Of Pope John Paul II

The Life And Messages Of Saint Faustina Kowalska

**Susan Crimp,
Sister Paulette Honeygosky, vsc.,
and Maxine Burton**

authorHOUSE®

AuthorHouse™
1663 Liberty Drive, Suite 200
Bloomington, IN 47403
www.authorhouse.com
Phone: 1-800-839-8640

First published by AuthorHouse 3/23/2010

ISBN: 978-1-4389-7747-8 (e)
ISBN: 978-1-4389-7745-4 (sc)
ISBN: 978-1-4389-7746-1 (hc)

Printed in the United States of America
Bloomington, Indiana

This book is printed on acid-free paper.

The book that you now hold represents the fulfillment of a lifelong dream of one of the greatest religious leaders of modern times. Throughout his life and particularly his distinguished papacy, Pope John Paul II was deeply devoted to Saint Faustina Kowalska: a woman he believed had received divine revelations from Christ. Included in these messages were instructions to have an image painted that all mankind should see. This same image has indeed been cited in conjunction with a number of miraculous occurrences. When a sufferer of Multiple Sclerosis prayed in front of this image for three days, he was able to stand up from his wheelchair and walk for the first time in years. Additionally, when passenger Fred Berretta sat in seat 16A, of the now famous 1549 flight which landed in the Hudson River, New York, he prayed to Saint Faustina as the plane was crashing. In fact, the accident occurred during the hour of 3.0'Clock, the precise time Christ had instructed Faustina to pray the words which He had given her. Today Fred Berretta believes Divine intervention saved everyone on board the US air flight that day. While years before Pope John Paul II wanted the whole world to see this image. The Pontiff believed it portrayed a true image of the coming Messiah.

Adding further credence to this story, throughout his papacy, Pope John Paul II made many declarations regarding the vital importance of this image and the messages imparted to Saint Faustina. Even the last moments of his life on this earth were spent celebrating *the Vigil of Divine Mercy*—a celebration that he himself instituted because of the messages that Faustina had received. Additionally, John Paul went to his final resting place with these messages in his casket, buried with his last homily, written on the day he died and on the subject of Faustina's revelations. Why were these messages so important to the late Pontiff? One of the reasons—many believe—is because Saint Faustina's messages contained specific mystical revelations concerning the last-days.

Yet, despite these facts, millions of people are entirely unaware of the high level of importance that the Pope placed on Faustina's Image and messages, and how they seemingly correlate with many of the events happening in our world today. Additionally, despite the late Pope's expressed desire and efforts to make this Image known throughout the world, it is still largely unseen—even in Catholic Churches. Therefore, in as much as the revelations and messages of Saint Faustina are uniquely communicated in these pages, the book that you are holding represents the fulfillment of one of Pope John Paul II's greatest dreams.

The overriding message of this book is a sober warning to the world, but also a message of great hope, as was evidenced by the miraculous landing of flight 1549. It is a hope that is needed now, perhaps more than ever—at a time when so many dark clouds seem to be hanging above a world in economic despair, plagued by deadly diseases including the so called 'swine flu' which have swept the world, and a moment in history where our world is in a violent conflict over religion and God. Consequently, this book, beyond representing the fulfillment of Pope John Paul II's expressed wishes, also represents a counterbalance to the evil and darkness that humanity has witnessed since the beginning of this 21st Century.

The Pope was well aware that on September 11th 1683, the Polish King, Jan Sobeiski, had gained a great victory defending Europe against the onslaught of the Islamic Ottoman Empire at Vienna. He also knew that on the very same day in 2001, Islamic fundamentalists had started the battle again, this time with a view toward global domination. Additionally, the subsequent rise in terrorism, war in the Middle East, and the unimaginable death tolls of both natural and man-made disasters have made us all think a bit more about our destinies and where our world is now heading.

Yet despite the darkness that we have all felt creeping over the earth, we are not a world without hope. Pope John Paul II began his papacy with the words "Be not afraid." The late pontiff became convinced that the messages sent to Faustina were given to reassure the world that despite all that may happen in the future, in the end, evil will not prevail, nor will it have the last word...

CONTENTS

FOREWORD

On the very day of his papal installation on October 22, 1978, the late Pontiff John Paul II told the world that the message that Jesus Christ had imparted to a woman named Faustina was not only authentic but would form the image and thrust of his remarkable pontificate. Who was Saint Faustina, you ask? She was the woman Christ called "His secretary"—a young humble nun, a simple uneducated woman, age thirty-three when she died in 1938, who was asked to prepare the world for Christ's return. Imagine how I felt when I learned that this woman, my cousin, was going to become a canonized Saint and had been deemed a modern day prophet by Pope John Paul II, a man many believe was one of the greatest theologians who ever lived. In the months that preceded her canonization ceremony, the occasion which formally recognized her sanctity that took place during the Easter of 2000, at St. Peter's in Rome, which I was privileged to attend, I learned much about Faustina's deeply spiritual journey. I was intrigued. In addition, I wondered then, even as I wonder now, about the inexplicable way in which she was led by grace and the Spirit within to trust, to believe, to respond, and to do, the will of God for her. Recently, in a world where there is now much violence and religious friction that threatens the future of the world, I was presented with the following interpretation of the life, writings, and mission of St. Faustina and their possible significance for the times we are living in. As I read this manuscript, and began working on it, I knew that it is a timely message of hope from God, sent at a time in history where there is much despair. It is a reminder, I believe, as did the late Pope John Paul II, that the messages given to St. Faustina- are intended for the whole world. However you believe, wherever you are, or are not, in your own spiritual journey, I invite you to read this story; in doing so the last wish of Pope John Paul II will be realized.

Sister Paulette Honeygosky, vsc

Introduction:

The Last Wish Of Pope John Paul II

Right from the beginning of my ministry in St. Peter's See in Rome, I considered this message my special task. Providence has assigned it to me in the present situation of man, the Church and the world.

—Pope John Paul II referring to the message found in *The Diary of Saint Faustina.*

We are now standing in the face of the greatest historical confrontation humanity has gone through. I do not think that wide circles of American society or wide circles of the Christian community realize this fully. We are now facing the final confrontation between the Church and the anti-Church, of the Gospel versus the anti-Gospel.

—Karol Cardinal Wojtyla (Pope John Paul II),
November 9, 1976

Vatican City 2005:

If ever there was a moment in history when the whole world seemed to gather in prayer, it was most certainly on April 2, 2005 as Pope John Paul II lay on his deathbed. The Pope's final hours were marked by the uninterrupted prayer of those assisting him, and others who had come to bid farewell to their dear friend. Throughout his seventeen year reign as Pope, the Papal Apartments had been John Paul's home. Located on the top floor of the Apostolic Palace, there are seven large rooms, a simple private chapel, an office, roof garden, as well as staff quarters for the nuns who run the Papal Household. Though the configuration has changed since the installation of Pope Benedict XVI in order to accommodate his large collection of books, this was how it was when John Paul II lived there. Additionally, the apartments also contained their own medical suite and it was there in this modified hospital facility where during the last hours of his life, John Paul made two final requests; to have the Bible read to him, and to celebrate the vigil Mass for the Feast of Divine Mercy.

There was indeed divine irony in the fact that the Pope would die on the eve of the very feast which he had devoted so much of his life promoting and which was so close to his heart. A celebration which the Pope believed was vital for the future of humanity. The Divine Mercy Feast had been reinstalled in the Church as a result of Saint Faustina, a woman who received divinely inspired messages and was instructed to share them specifically to prepare the world for the return of the Messiah.

While such claims might seem dramatic and perhaps even quite dubious to many, Pope John Paul II most certainly believed these claims with all of his heart. Additionally, despite the fact that even many within the echelons of the Catholic Church viewed this woman's testimony with skepticism, it was nevertheless their most beloved Pope who made Saint Faustina the first Catholic Saint of this millennium.

John Paul also fully understood the importance of the enigmatic *Image of Divine Mercy*—an "icon" or an Image of Christ that Faustina saw in a vision, which she was specifically commissioned to have painted. The Image portrays Christ standing and making the sign of blessing. Additionally, proceeding forth from Christ's heart are two rays of light—white and red—representing the blood and the water that burst forth from his heart on the cross. While the Image is now found in some churches around the world, even to this day, many both inside and outside the Catholic Church do not understand the deeper prophetic significance of the Image of Divine Mercy.

It was at 20.00 hours when the Pope's dying wish began to be realized. The mass dedicated to celebrate Saint Faustina's revelations, which Christ had asked to be installed in the annual Church calendar, began to be celebrated in his private apartment. At this most solemn moment it seemed fitting that the ailing pontiff was given the *Holy Viaticum* and the *Sacrament of Anointing of the Sick*, commonly known as the last rites. Then, as the Mass concluded, an instant later John Paul II had gone home to be with the Lord. It was 21.37, local time in Rome. At that moment 13 people—old friends and aides from his native Poland, as well as his Italian doctors and nurses— witnessed the end of an era. As the room swelled with emotion, Archbishop Stanislaw Dziwisz, John Paul's most trusted personal secretary who had never left the Pontiff's deathbed, held the Pope's hand as Polish nuns recited the Rosary through tears. The reign of arguably the most famous Pope in the two thousand year history of the Church had come to an end.

Today following his death and in light of the late pontiff's devotion to the Divine Mercy messages given to St. Faustina, many now call Pope John Paul "the Mercy Pope." The late Pontiff wanted to let the whole world have access to these messages and to the Image. To date, several books have been written which attempt to expound the meaning of Faustina's messages of mercy, but none have been written with a special emphasis on *the Image of Divine Mercy* that Christ commissioned Faustina to have painted. It was an Image that according to Faustina's diary would help to prepare the world for His return. Beyond this, there has not been any specific treatment of *the Image* and how it relates to many of the very frightening events that we are now witnessing in the world. This book makes every effort to fulfill this task with the greatest care. This discussion of God's mercy and Christ's return comes at the perfect time. It is presented at a juncture in history when the world is locked in a conflict over God. Indeed by June 2007, this conflict had reached such a bloody crescendo that a Report released by Britain's intelligence service MI6 revealed an estimated 200 million Christians in 60 countries are now facing persecution. The report was sent to Pope Benedict and Church leaders and was the first time the British secret intelligence service has shared its information with religious leaders. "We do so because we believe the situation is extremely serious," said an MI6 source. The news came just as Hamas had become Israel's neighbor in Gaza, and began warning Christians in the region that they must embrace Islam.

This book will explore the unique prophetic significance of the messages and the Image as they relate specifically to many of the events we are witnessing throughout the world today.

PART ONE:

THE WOMAN WHO
INTERVIEWED CHRIST

CHAPTER ONE

HUMBLE BEGINNINGS

"You will prepare the world for my final coming."
—**Diary Entry 429**

If you have faith, the notion that Christ would impart messages in a Diary to warn the world of His final coming may not seem at all preposterous and no explanation as to why Christ might have sent these messages to be revealed at the start of the 21st century is necessary. Indeed, in addition to the international tensions over the Middle East conflict, what humanity has witnessed since the start of the new millennium is almost beyond comprehension with terror attacks in the name of Islam in virtually every corner of the globe. This is also the century that saw Sister Faustina Kowalska become its first Canonized Saint. If, on the other hand, you do not have faith, it is conceivable that no explanation is possible. Yet even when examining the story of Faustina from a skeptical perspective, it is very difficult to get past several facts. Additionally, regardless of one's religious or non-religious belief, it is very difficult not to believe that our world at this juncture in history is desperately in need of hope and much prayer.

Nevertheless, why would humanity need an Image, with the inscription "Jesus I trust in you" as well as a prayer asking for God's Mercy to be sanctioned by the Vatican specifically in April 2000? After all, on the face of it there have been thousands of different icons and images of Christ presented over the Centuries. Why is this one any different? Could it be that this Image, which Christ Himself instructed Faustina to have painted, represents the true face of the coming messiah? Why is it that when this Image is superimposed onto the Shroud of Turin that it provides a precise match? Do recent World events suggest that mankind is on a downward spiral and might possibly need divine reassurance? Could this possibly explain why these messages were sent to u's for revelation now? Furthermore, is this all a divine mystery that could only be more fully revealed at this particular moment in time when we might better need and understand it?

Let us consider some facts about what has happened to our World since the turn of the 21st Century. All of us are horribly aware where we were on September 11, 2001 when America was attacked by Islamic fundamentalists. Now, all these years later it is still almost impossible to fully comprehend the death toll on that day—calculated to be over 2,900. The events that unfolded following September 11th are equally terrifying. The wars in Afghanistan and Iraq as well as the countless terror attacks all over the world including Bali, Madrid, London, Russia, Pakistan, China and Israel—along with the ongoing conflict in the Middle East, as well as a world in economic turmoil. There is it seems that no area of the world is immune from tragedy, and ever increasing natural tragedies have also given us cause for concern. In Iran on December 26, 2003, a major earthquake registering 6.5 on the Richter scale hit the southeastern province of Bam, killing 43,000 people and injuring thousands of others, leaving an estimated 75,000 people homeless. Disaster struck again exactly one year later in 2004 in South East Asia in the Indian Ocean tsunami, and even now officials still don't know exactly how many people died. A tally of conservative government figures puts the number of dead and missing at more than 216,000 in 11 countries. August 2005, saw Hurricane Katrina hit America taking around 1,033 lives in its path. Two months later, in October 2005, over 80,000 people were lost in an earthquake in Pakistan. While in May, 2008 a cyclone of mammoth proportions claimed hundreds of thousands of lives in Burma, and a massive earthquake left an equally horrifying death toll in China.

Then at the beginning of 2010 an Earthquake in Haiti caused unimaginable pain and suffering. While Chile also suffered a devastating earth shift too.

There are also other forces at work which also pose a threat to the security of the world. In Iran, President Mahmoud Ahmadinejad believes he must bring about the end-times and pave the way for the return of the Shi'a Muslim Messiah figure known as Imam al-Mahdi. Ordinarily such statements would be dismissed as the ranting of a madman. Clearly though, Ahmadinejad's power on the world stage cannot be ignored. Iran has a large proportion of the world's oil supply and can threaten to hold the world ransom.

Given that the Islamic Republic of Iran also continues to pursue its nuclear program, all the while voicing his opinion that Israel should cease to exist as a nation, we have a right to be concerned that its leader is waiting for his apocalyptic so-called *Messiah*.

In fact a majority of Muslims believe the "12th Iman" or Mahdi, an Islamic messianic figure, was placed in hiding until *al-Qiyama* or "The Day of Judgment". There is much dissent among Muslim factions as to who this savior figure will be and where and when he will return. Some factions even believe this Mahdi may be Jesus himself. However, almost all Muslims agree that in order for this day to arrive, Israel must be destroyed. A chilling thought considering that in June 2007 radical Islamic extremists took over Gaza leaving Israel with a radical Islamic neighbor that wishes to destroy her.Additionally, Iranian President Mahmoud Ahmadinejad has been cited by various news sources as not only believing in the eventual return of the Mahdi, but that the return is near and that it is the responsibility of the Iranian government to prepare the country for the occasion. The Iranian President's anticipation of the 12th Imam and his call for his return along with his derogatory religious rhetoric towards the nation of Israel is certainly a far cry from the belief system of the views of the late Pope John Paul II, whose funeral the Iranian President ironically attended. Certainly the Iranian's comments regarding his denial of the Holocaust and the elimination of the State of Israel are totally against the mindset of any rational or God-fearing human being, and certainly contrary to the late Holy Father; who believed in the Divine Mercy of God and the exhibiting of love to all the people of the world regardless of their belief system. Whichever way we confront the issue, fundamentalist

5

Islam is at war with Christians, Jews and apparently anyone not of its same mindset, including peaceful Muslims. A position polar opposite to Pope John Paul II who spent his life exhibiting love to all people and who made a point of visiting every corner of the world to express his concern for the entire human family. This desire to show love came as a result of a call from God, compassion from birth and also as a direct result of messages contained in *Saint Faustina's Diary: Divine Mercy in My Soul*. Could it be that, just as Joan of Arc was given a divine mission from God so many centuries ago, so also has Faustina Kowalska been commissioned to spiritually prepare the world for the great difficulties that may lie ahead?

This was certainly a notion that had occurred to Pope John Paul II when he stated that he wanted the message of *The Diary* known to the whole world. Current world events seem to bear out the need for this. The US government was trying to establish a new anti-missile site in Europe designed to stop attacks by Iran against the United States and its European allies. In a twist of irony the location was going to be Poland. In one of the dictations in *The Diary* Christ talks to Faustina about her native land.

> *I bear a special love for Poland, and if she will be obedient to My will, I will exalt her in might and holiness. From her will come forth the spark that will prepare the world for my final coming.*

> **—Diary entry 1732**

International concerns over the nuclear issue were highlighted as of September 2006, when Russia and Iran signed a deal in Moscow envisaging the launch of Iran's nuclear reactor very soon. Fears were also heightened when Russian troops stormed into Georgia in 2008.

It is sadly true that new tensions are emerging throughout the world daily. Yet while this may bring with it a certain measure of fear, it is quite evident that Faustina's Diary and its message are perfectly suited for such a time as this, not only to give us hope, but also to confirm to us that evil will not have the last word. The messages come above all to reassure us that a merciful and just God is indeed in charge and He is watching over us all. Indeed, Pope John Paul II, was well aware of the vital importance of the messages and the Image, and was determined that everyone on earth should know about them. Yet, the question remains as to why would the most famous Pope that ever lived would stake his impeccable reputation on these messages?

Could it be that this is all part of the Divine plan unfolding according to a Divine timetable?

In fact whether you are a person of faith or not, it is certainly interesting to note that even the greatest scientist who ever lived, the man who single-handedly invented modern science, Sir Issac Newton, was certain that the entire universe and even the Bible itself, was a "cryptogram set by the Almighty"—a puzzle which God had made, meant to be solved by man. Modern science was not enough however for Newton—he also believed we needed ancient wisdom to solve the ultimate mysteries. After his death, when Newton's writings were discovered at Cambridge University, they contained millions of words about ancient civilizations, and details of a code in the Bible and the Apocalypse.

More recently newly discovered writings of Newton reveal he believed the world could end in 2060. Whether his findings are accurate remains to be seen. What we do know is that a simple nun was given instructions to prepare the world for the final coming of Christ and Pope John Paul II believed her. It is our hope that this book will demonstrate to the soul with an open mind and heart that all of the pieces of Faustina's enigmatic and puzzling life and message as well as the long process of canonization that followed, can be seen to all flow and fit together quite beautifully to form for us a picture of an infinitely merciful and loving God who is reaching out to all of mankind in the midst of a very troubled age. A time in history when Islamic fundamentalists are asking us to reconsider who the God of the Bible actually is? Maybe now is the right time to know the story of Saint Faustina and her messages.

Indeed, if Faustina's messages have been sent for global revelation to us at this time then it is indeed prophetic.

We are after all in a world turned upside down and involved in religious differences. Should we therefore consider the possibility of Divine timing, and also the most important role of Divine providence? Many in the highest echelons of the Vatican had no choice but to put the revelations of St. Faustina into the category of Divine origin, because as they investigated Faustina's revelations, they concluded mere coincidence could not provide all of the necessary answers.

Why were two people who had never met—both from Poland—one a Pope, the other a humble nun able to help bring these messages to the World? Is it part of a Divine plan or is it all a mere coincidence? Even the theological study conducted to validate or dismiss Faustina states: If the revelation didn't come from God but were the product of a morbid imagination or the result of illusion created by a malevolent Spirit, Helena Faustina would have been an unlikely person.

Now, as the story of Faustina's spiritual journey unfolds, new light can be shed on the significance of current news events and *The Diary* and maybe help to explain why Pope John Paul II wanted everyone to know the messages and see the Image imparted to her. For the moment however, it is important to understand who Faustina was, what drew her to Christ. Additionally we shall discover what made her open to receive these instructions and why God chose her.

It all begins with the story of a simple woman who chose a life of service to God but ultimately becomes the receiver of Divine messages and an Image sent to be shared with all mankind.

Given the mammoth task assigned to her, it is interesting that in light of her humble and poverty-stricken background, Helena Kowalska never even saw a newspaper as a child. Indeed this is quite ironic given the enormity of what she was expected to undertake for humanity and also considering that, following her death, she became not only a major story at the Vatican, but also the instrument that formed the papacy of the most famous and media friendly Pope in history.

Faustina's ultimate journey all seems a million miles away from the early years of this young woman's life. The little girl baptized Helena Kowalska would one day become known as Saint Faustina. Today Poland, a devoutly Catholic nation, is the destination for millions of pilgrims from all over the world who travel to pray at the National Shrine of Our Lady of Czestochowa, the tomb of Saint Faustina and the childhood home of Pope John Paul II. The country is now a member of the European Community and Poles have a tremendous sense of patriotic pride and optimism about their future. It is indeed a very different landscape from the country that baby Helen Kowalska was born into on August 25, 1905.

To describe the Kowalska family as poor would be an understatement. Despite their material poverty however, they were abundantly rich in their Catholic faith. Their home—a tiny stone cottage comprised of two bedrooms—made living conditions somewhat cramped for ten children and their parents. Aside from their faith, there was nothing which set the Kowalska's apart from any other struggling family in the tiny village, unknown to the rest of the world. Even today, the obscure village of Glogoweic is of such little consequence to Poland that the birthplace of one of the country's greatest Saints does not even feature on maps of the country but merely makes up part of the town of Swinice Warickie. Although Faustina's life would pass by without respect or recognition, from the moment she was born her mother Marianna believed she was different. This fact is confirmed by her mother's statement following Faustina's birth: That blessed Child sanctified my womb". This comment was not repeated at the births of Faustina's siblings. Clearly from the moment of her birth there was something special about her. Something, which evident by the comment she made, even her Mother believed was direct from God. This was not just an emotional response to the birth of a child. In fact, her mother was grateful for the birth of a healthy baby because prior to Faustina her mother had endured two extremely painful pregnancies and two of her other children had died in infancy. Indeed, there are no documented references which refer to the holiness of her other children.

Of course, she loved them equally, but Mrs. Kowalska clearly sensed that there was something different about young Helena. Indeed, the entire family seemed rather special, because while their life was one of constant struggle not even their extreme poverty could sway their faith and trust in God. Indeed the Kowalska's piety was quite remarkable in light of the fact that they appeared to have very little else. According to Faustina's official biographer and the woman responsible for translating The Diary into English, one of the world's foremost experts on Faustina and her messages, Sister Sophia Michalenko, the Kowalska's lived off the land but the soil was far from fertile. "In the poor soil, only potatoes and rye grew with any success. There were also pastures on which cows were allowed to graze, but only after the second haying." The backdrop of the nation did not appear to help either. Poland faced great unrest at the turn of the 20th century as a result of a poor economy and with the constant threat of revolutionary unrest and general strikes. While Faustina's father owned a number of acres of land, the income was not enough to support ten children. Industrious and devoted, Stanislaus would supplement his income by working as a carpenter. It is interesting to note that many of the Saints of the Church, especially the seers and visionaries including Bernadette at Lourdes, the Fatima children and of course Joan of Arc, would also suffer as a result of poverty in childhood. The other common denominator was their unequivocal trust in God. While young Helena's faith came from God, there can be no doubt that it was also positively reinforced by her parents, especially by her father, who despite the tremendous financial pressures he faced, could frequently be heard in the family home uttering the words, "The first duty is to God". Her Father would never miss Mass on Sunday and even in old age, when he was bedridden and his health would not allow him to attend services, he would hang his watch over the bed and participate spiritually. Her parent's piety was a trait Helena would inherit. As soon as she was able to speak, she could be heard reciting short prayers at home. The faith of Faustina's family was simply extremely strong. Life as a child was very difficult for young Helena but she was determined to battle on regardless of what obstacles came her way. This training would hold her in good stead for her mission on earth, which was to persuade the Catholic Church that Jesus had a message for all mankind, a message for believers and nonbelievers.

Reading her diary, it is evident that Faustina experienced the call to follow Christ in childhood.

> *From the age of seven, I experienced the definite call of God, the grace of a vocation to the religious life. It was the first time I heard God's voice in my soul; that is, an invitation to a perfect life*

> —**Diary entry 7**

Yet in childhood young Helena's exterior life was far from perfect and things were not easy behind the walls of the Kowalska family home. Not only was there barely enough food on the table, but also few clothes to wear. At one point, so hard was the plight of this struggling family that Sister Sophia recalls; Once World War I began, all of Poland suffered destruction, great famine, and poverty. The Kowalska family was almost destitute; they could not afford the proper clothing to attend Church. This caused Faustina much grief. When she could not go to Mass on Sunday because she had no dress to wear and her sisters would take turns wearing the one dress they possessed between them, young Helena would take her prayer book and find a suitable hiding place to pray while the Mass was being celebrated in the nearby Church.

Yet it seemed neither lack of food or clothing or a sense of poverty could interfere with this young girl's devotion to God—a trait she exhibited in her charity towards others.

Neighbors were often flabbergasted as they witnessed this six-year-old girl's kindness and generosity towards those less fortunate. Indeed this young girl, whose religious name would later, become Faustina, which means fortunate or blessed, could best be described in her childhood as an infant version of Mother Teresa. In fact, her childhood acts of charity and compassion given her own life circumstance never ceased to amaze those around her.

Frequently she would create her own version of a store, make paper cut out dolls and sell them, giving all the proceeds to the poor even though her own family could have certainly benefited from the money. Faustina however always thought of others—a characteristic that certainly attracted the attention of the other children in the village, many of whom followed her around hoping to hear one of the many religious stories she had learned from her father. Indeed her cheerful disposition gave no indication of the horror of famine and war that surrounded her.

Faustina's family's financial plight did not ease up at any time in her childhood. There was however no indication of bitterness or anger. Poland did not see an increase in prosperity, putting great financial struggle on this devoted family of ten. Yet despite their own hardships, nothing would weaken this family's faith and for Faustina, her family's poverty merely served to firmly establish her union with God and make her completely dependent and connected to Him.

A troubled childhood was not exclusive to Faustina. In the lives of many Saints of the Catholic Church their early years were often marked with tragedy, ill health and in some cases visions. It is indeed interesting to note the courage and sufferings many Holy men and women of the Church had to endure.

Today St. Teresa of Avila is considered one of the greatest mystics of all time. She is a Doctor of the Catholic Church and her writings are the source of great inspiration centuries after they were written. Yet when she was only seven she had a strong desire for martyrdom, and wanted to see God. Persuading her brother Rodrigo they would have to die first to achieve their goal the two set forth hand in hand at an early hour in the morning to seek the desired martyrdom. Luckily an uncle spotted the pair and took them home. Teresa with earnest eyes repeated her assertion: "I wanted to go to God, and one cannot do that unless one dies first."   St Bernadette Soubirous the French nun made famous for her apparitions at Lourdes also suffered with an asthma condition in childhood. The illness would ultimately cause her so much suffering that in the convent, she would beg the nuns to tear open her chest so that she might breathe. In fact, another French Saint, Joan of Arc also endured suffering. It was around 1424, at the age of 12, when Joan said she began to have visions of Saints Catherine and Margaret (two early Christian martyrs) and St. Michael the Archangel (identified in the Bible as the commander of Heaven's armies who led the war against Satan). Just like Joan of Arc, Faustina too exhibited a strong connection to the supernatural in childhood and could be overheard reciting prayers, and claimed to have received dreams of a supernatural nature. Young Helena described one dream to her Mother: "I was walking hand in hand with the Mother of God in a beautiful garden." Something was clearly happening in the soul of young Faustina. On other occasions, even before she had reached the age of seven, she would awaken at night, and sit upright in bed, quite obviously in prayer and thus alarmed her parents. Concerned about her young daughter not getting enough sleep, her mother would caution her. "Go back to sleep or you'll lose your mind." "Oh no Mother", she would answer, "My Guardian Angel must be waking me to pray."By the age of nine, as Faustina prepared to receive the sacraments of confession and Holy Communion, her night prayers increased which added to her parent's concern for their young daughter's health. Retrospectively however this might be seen as the beginning of her unique communion with God and the initial dialogue that would ultimately come to the attention of The Vatican and become a major part of Pope John Paul II's incredible Papacy.

Faustina often talked of these supernatural encounters with her parents, and once told of how she saw strange bright lights. Worried that such talk might cause some to question her sanity, her parents forbade her to talk about such nonsense. All in all this would be a rather ironic preparation for this young girl who would live a life where she would become a victim of much suspicion. Observing her in infancy this could be seen as just an innocent child with a devotion to God, but as she reached maturity, her visions became a matter of concern to those around her. After all, many were asking why she was singled out to receive these visions.

Yet there was never a question about Faustina's piety. Her devotion to God was evident to everyone. On the day of her first Holy Communion, before leaving home, she kissed the hand of both her parents and expressed sorrow for any small sins she may have committed against them. From this moment on she would attend confession every week and always kiss her parent's hands in preparation. This was a trait unique to Faustina and one that her siblings never imitated. It seemed as if Faustina had a Holy instinct all her own. She also never wanted to miss Sunday Mass and fitted in her household chores to ensure that she never did. Sister Sophia recalls how Faustina was a dutiful daughter in every area: "Helen helped around the house as soon as she was able to do so, putting things in order, and helping in the kitchen; later, she took care of the younger children and encouraged them to be obedient and diligent in the work they were told to do."

While this obedient daughter would always hold Sunday in special reverence as the Lord's Day, she never shunned her obligation to her family. Prior to Mass, she was often seen milking the cows in order to make sure her other family members had enough time to get to Church. Whenever it was her turn to take the cows to pasture, all the local children would follow her, each one of them awaiting a unique story about God or the Saints of the Church. Most of what Faustina read was done on her own. In light of the Russian occupation, most of the schools in Poland were closed for much of her childhood and school records show that she only began attending school at the age of twelve.

Unlike many of the other children, Faustina could read, and was a very enthusiastic student but due to her family's financial circumstances was never able to enjoy a full education. During the few winters that she was able to afford tuition however, Faustina received favorable reviews and was even found winning a competition for the recitation of Adam Mickiewicz's poem *Powrot Taty* (The Father's Return). Mickiewicz is regarded as Poland's greatest romantic poet though the Lithuanian's have also laid claim to him. After only three terms in the spring of 1919, Faustina and all the older students had to leave the cramped school to make way for the younger children and so she returned to work at home in order to help support her family.

Faustina had no regrets concerning the curtailing of her education. She knew she needed to help her family financially. Mentally she had already begun mapping out her future life of prayer. In the meantime, the Kowalska's needed food on the table and this dutiful daughter would try everything to help. It was quite evident that all she wanted to do when she didn't have household duties to attend to was to pray. Faustina was well aware that she had a call from God and needed to answer it—she just did not know where. The hardships of her family's economic situation meanwhile began to take their toll. As Sister Michalenko recalls:It was in the spring of 1921, fifteen- year- old Helen said to her mother, "Mom, Daddy works so hard and yet I still have nothing to wear. Of all the girls, I have the worst looking dress. I should be going out to earn something for myself."

Faustina was clearly not just acting out of material concern; she felt a genuine need to help provide for her family. Having already allowed her two eldest daughters to work as housekeepers, her mother, Marianna gave her approval. "Well then my child, go in the name of God." Ever obedient Faustina, having received her mother's blessing quickly found work at the home of Mrs. Helen Goryszewska, a sister of the Kowalska family's neighbor. The sense of responsibility Faustina was acquiring would also help her gain the necessary traits to cooperate with the Divine Plan awaiting her. She clearly had faith, and obedience to God's call. Furthermore, this dutiful daughter had demonstrated in childhood a willingness to listen to the word of God even if it meant being ridiculed or reprimanded. This childhood ability to trust in God would ultimately provide excellent training for the moment when Faustina would have to persuade the Church that Christ had a message for mankind. A message given exclusively to her to help prepare the world for His final coming!

Chapter Two

Unanswered Call

How long shall I put up with you and how long will
you keep putting me off.

—Jesus to Faustina, Diary entry 9

Faustina proved to be a valuable addition to The Goryszewska family and was not only a wonderful housekeeper but also a natural babysitter to Helen Goryszewka's young son. For hours on end the young child would sit mesmerized by Faustina's stories and his natural mother felt quite comfortable leaving the little one with her most trusted employee. Within a short time came the heartbreaking news that Faustina had to move on, which left Mrs. Goryszewka feeling both saddened and perplexed. "Why are you leaving." She asked the young woman who had quickly become like a member of the family. Faustina's reply failed to offer any explanation, "I can't stay any longer." With which she gave up her only way of supporting herself. Clearly what her devastated employer could not see from the outside was that Faustina was interiorly being called by God. For even though she had dutifully attended to her job with great obedience and cleaned the home and looked after the child as if it was her own, unbeknown to all around her Faustina spent much time silently praying throughout the day. At night meanwhile she found herself absorbed by a strange brightness which kept her awake. It was a hidden life she could no longer conceal. Realizing she could no longer stay in the world Faustina decided to quit her job and asked her mother's permission to join a convent.

As direct and to the point as Faustina was in asking "Mother, I must enter the convent," so too was the flat and out and out rejection of both her parents to the idea. Her father blamed their refusal on the family's economic circumstances but clearly neither parent wanted to see their favorite daughter disappear from their lives. "I have no money for a dowry and I still have unpaid bills," was the reply from Faustina's father. His dutiful daughter on the other hand could not understand the obstacle, "Daddy, I don't need money, Jesus himself will lead me to a convent." Yet despite the strong faith of both her mother and father, it seemed that neither of them was prepared to hand Faustina over to God.

Devastated by her parent's reaction Faustina was torn. This obedient young woman could not disobey her parents but she knew she had to go with God. Reluctantly she decided to face the world again. It was a difficult decision to leave her parents' home and go live with her cousins but Faustina thought it was necessary. Luckily she found employment working for three women who belonged to The Third Order of St Francis, and Faustina was at least able to maintain a life of prayer. Faustina's schedule allowed her to attend daily Mass and also visit the sick and dying. These acts of charity became the brunt of jokes amongst her cousins and uncle who could not understand why a young woman would worry about such things. Faustina was adamant about her vocation. "I will go and serve God because that is what I resolve to do since my childhood and that I will do." Again the inner voice started to call her and again she asked her parents' permission. Even though Faustina begged her parents they would still not concede. It became a very sad moment in her life and she would later record in her diary that it made her try and become like any other young woman, and abandon her dream of religious life and the role God had intended for her.

> *The eighteenth year of my life. An earnest appeal to my parents for permission to enter the convent. My parents' flat refusal, I turned myself over to the vain things of life, paying no attention to the call of grace, although my soul found no satisfaction in any of these things. The incessant call of grace caused me much anguish; I tried, however,*

to stifle it with amusements. Interiorly, I shunned God, turning with all my heart to creatures. However God's grace won out in my soul.

—Diary entry 8

On February 2, 1923, seemingly resolved to carry out a life in the world, Faustina found work through an employment agency in the house of Mrs. Sadowska. In somewhat of an ironic twist the young woman, who as a child did not have a dress to wear to Mass, was so well turned out for the job interview, her future employer almost did not want to hire her. "Helen came to me so fashionably dressed that I hesitated to hire her as a maid. I purposely lowered the amount of salary so that she would go away but Helen accepted my proposition." Retrospectively her employer was pleased she did. Marianna Sadowska was a grocery store owner and often had to be away from her three children for extended periods of time. Faustina meanwhile acted as a most reliable housekeeper and babysitter, who kept the children amused for hours on end with her vibrant personality and wonderful sense of humor. Another aspect of her character which endeared her to the family was Faustina's strong observance of faith. She never ate meat on Wednesday, Friday or Saturday and during lent never ate meat at all, She also was a regular participant in services at the Cathedral.

Even though she was able to survive very well in the world Faustina was still consumed by the call to religious life. Knowing that she could not live this way much longer Faustina said goodbye to the Sadowska's and left her position on July 1, 1924. Though devastated by the departure Mrs. Sadowska recalled how it was done with love and concern for the family she had become very much a part of. "She would have left sooner but she was so good and caring, I knew she waited until my baby was born."

It was at this juncture that Faustina was soon to experience the beginning of her most profound communications with Christ. Encounters which, following years of skepticism from the Church, were ultimately authenticated. Indeed, there were grounds to be somewhat suspicious of what Faustina claimed to have happened, and if the experience had happened to anyone else it would have been met with disbelief. However in Faustina's case it would be one of many encounters she said she had with

Jesus. As she recounted the episodes to her superiors all of a sudden in the most unlikely of places Faustina claimed to have seen a vision that would forever change her life. The reports of these visions would ultimately change the life of Pope John Paul II. Yet, while few people within the Vatican would listen to the story of Saint Faustina and her messages, when John Paul II became Pope everything changed. On the face of it, it is quite difficult to understand what happened to Faustina, but it would become a moment she would later recall in her dairy.

> *Once I was at a dance with one of my sisters. While everybody was having a good time, my soul was experiencing deep torments. As I began to dance, I suddenly saw Jesus at my side, Jesus racked with pain, stripped of His clothing, all covered with wounds, who spoke these words to me: How long shall I put up with you and how long will you keep putting Me off? At that moment the charming music stopped {and} the company I was with vanished from my sight; pretending to have a headache in order to cover up what took place in my soul. After a while I slipped out unnoticed, leaving my sister and all my companions behind and made my way to the Cathedral of Saint Stanislaus Kostka. It was almost twilight; there were only a few people in the cathedral. Paying no attention to what was happening around me. I fell prostrate before the Blessed Sacrament and begged the Lord to be good enough to give me to understand what I should do next. Then I heard these words: Go at once to Warsaw; you will enter a convent there. I rose from prayer, came home, and took care of things that needed to be settled. As best I could I confided to my sister what took place within my soul.*

> **—Diary entry 9**

What is interesting to note is the fact that while her instructions from Christ cannot be proven it is clear that Faustina carried them out and would ultimately become a canonized Saint. At this point in her life however she was a fragile young woman who desperately wanted to follow her heart and what she believed was The Will of God.

Faustina started to pack a few possessions, said goodbye to her sister and proceeded on to her Uncle's home to break the news. "I am going to Warsaw to enter a convent," she said. Furious her uncle warned her of what effect such a plan would have on her parents. "You know this will make your dear mother and father very sad and break their hearts." A determined Faustina would not be moved; "Well then Uncle, tell them nothing now. When you do get to visit them later give them these clothes." The flabbergasted man seemed perplexed. "And what will you have?" He asked. "What I am wearing is enough. Jesus will take care of all my needs." She said. At which point her reluctant uncle took her to the train station. Though Faustina managed to maintain her composure as she bid the man she loved goodbye, she would recall years later that she was inwardly as heartbroken and frightened as her family.

> *In my one dress, with no other belongings, I arrived in Warsaw. When I got off the train and saw that all were going their separate ways, I was overcome with fear. What am I to do? To whom should I turn, as I know no one? So I said to the Mother of God, "Mary, lead me guide, me.*
>
> — **Diary entry 10**

All a sudden Faustina who had previously started to receive messages from Christ was now in communication with the Mother of God.

> *Immediately I heard these words within me telling me to leave the town and to go to a certain nearby village where I would find safe lodging for the night. I did so and found, in fact, that everything was just as the Mother of God told me.*
>
> —**Diary entry 11**

The next morning in the nearby village she had gone to at the instruction of the message and now clearly motivated by the reinforced trust in God Faustina headed back into the city and entered the first Church she saw, St James at Grojecka Street in Ochota, a suburb of Warsaw. It was here that Faustina began to pray in order to determine the will of God.

As she sat through one Holy Mass after another, at one point she heard the words. ***"Go to that Priest and tell him everything; he will tell you what to do next."*** (Diary entry 12)

While some may find it hard to believe these instructions again it is important to remember the ultimate outcome of Faustina's mission and obedience to the Divine plan.

Following the Mass Faustina carried out the instruction and went to the Priest. It is interesting that Father James Dabrowski listened intently to this stranger and was quite convinced of what she claimed had happened in her soul. Faustina then asked him where she should take the veil, and in what religious Order. Somewhat surprised by the young woman's desire he told Faustina to have strong confidence and assured her that God would provide for her future. As Faustina recounted the meeting in her diary entry. "For the time being," he said, "I shall send you to a pious lady {Aldona Lipszycowa} with whom you will stay until you enter the convent." It was an invitation that greatly helped Faustina who at this point was without a home in Warsaw.

> *When I called on the lady she received me very kindly. During the time I stayed with her, I was looking for a convent, but at whatever convent door I knocked, I was turned away. Sorrow gripped my heart, and I said to the Lord Jesus, "Help me: don't leave me alone".*

> **—Diary entry 13**

One can only imagine what was going through her mind and in the mind of anyone around her. Here she believed she was listening to Christ and no one would take her in. This was certainly a test of faith and eventually after being turned away from convent upon convent each one of which regarded her as poorly educated, Faustina in despair turned to Jesus. **"Help me do not leave me alone."** Eventually her prayers were answered but there were further obstacles to overcome. As she knocked on the door of Our Lady of Mercy at 3/9 Zytnia Street Faustina had fear pounding in her heart. Opening the door the portress took one look at her and enquired, "What do you want, my child?" "I wish to enter the convent," Faustina replied. She was then instructed to come in and wait for the Superior. Unbeknownst to Faustina as she waited patiently Mother Michael Moraczewska was secretly observing the young woman and based on her appearance alone was seriously thinking of sending her away. Mother

Michael, spoke several languages and had attended the Conservatory of Music. Entering the convent later in life, she was considered to be highly educated for those times and used the gifts she had gathered in the world to help develop the spiritual and mental aspects of the community.

Though from vastly different educational backgrounds, upon talking to the young Helena, Mother Michael was impressed by her maturity and pleasant and charitable disposition and told her to go to the convent chapel and ask Jesus what He wanted of her. Faustina, with great joy proceeded to the chapel and asked Jesus: "Lord of this house, do you accept me?" According to her Diary the response was immediate. "I heard this voice: *"I do accept you; you are in my Heart."* (Diary entry 14) When I returned to the chapel, Mother Superior asked first of all, "Well, has the Lord accepted you?" I answered, "Yes." It was a moment of great joy for Faustina; finally she was accepted into The Congregation of the Sisters of Our Lady of Mercy. A religious community founded by Teresa Rondeau in 1818, and brought to Poland by Countess Potocka in 1862. The main purpose of the community is to provide Mercy to all types of misery facing humanity with a special concern for the rehabilitation of wayward women and girls.

Even though accepted by the congregation the road of entry into the convent would still prove bumpy. Without any dowry she would have to continue working and save the money. Once again Faustina rose to the challenge with humility and devotion.

Over the next few months continuing with her same employer Faustina saved money and sent it to Mother Michael. Sadly the superior had completely forgotten about Faustina when the envelope arrived. Faustina meanwhile kept working and striving to answer God's call. There would be one last ditch effort from her sister Genevieve who traveled to Warsaw to try and talk her out of religious life, and to go back home but this time Faustina would not concede. Resolute to follow the will of God and the voices she was hearing. On the eve of the Feast of Our Lady of the Angels, August 1st, 1925 Helena Kowalska entered the convent. It was a moment she would later describe of tremendous joy.

> *"I felt immensely happy; it seemed to me that I had stepped into a life of paradise, A single prayer bursting forth from my heart, one of thanksgiving."*

> **(Diary entry 17)**

Chapter Three

Convent Life

"It is you who will cause Me this pain if you leave the convent."

—Jesus to Sister Faustina —Diary entry 19

If ever the phrase, "Be careful what you wish for," could be applied to Faustina's life, it would surely have occurred to her upon joining The Congregation of the Sisters of Our Lady of Mercy. Within days of her convent entry, this woman who had pinned all of her hopes on living the religious life felt entirely disillusioned. It is impossible to know just exactly how she had envisaged life in the convent, but it is evident in her struggles to adapt that Faustina had something entirely different in mind.

Indeed, one of the many reasons Pope John Paul II took Faustina so seriously was in addition to her obvious piety her life was a constant struggle and far from being viewed as a saint many treated her with skepticism. Yet she was quite sincere and it was because of her desire to live a life of total service to God that she found her particular convent not as authentic as she had imagined.

What is known from her diary and other accounts is that Faustina had imagined a place with a much stronger emphasis on prayer and contemplation. As a result, this woman who had struggled so much and overcome so many obstacles to join a convent was suddenly overcome by a strong temptation to leave. Making matters worse, it was impossible to discuss the situation with the Mother Superior and so Faustina was left to struggle alone.

Forever strong in faith, Faustina fervently prayed to know God's will. Then one day in her cell (an individual's room in a convent or monastery is referred to as *a cell*), she received her answer. "After a while brightness filled my cell, and on the curtain I saw the very sorrowful face of Jesus. There were opened wounds on His Face, and large tears were falling on my bedspread. Not knowing what all this meant, I asked Jesus, "Jesus, who has hurt You so?" And Jesus said to me, *"It is you who will cause Me this pain if you leave the convent. It is to this place that I have called you and nowhere else; and I have prepared many graces for you."* (Diary entry 19) I begged pardon of Jesus and immediately changed my decision." After talking with a priest the next day to whom she confided the encounter, Faustina ever obedient to God's will, decided to stay and put all self doubt behind her.

Faustina's initial role in the community was a combination of kitchen duty and cleaning the room of Mother Jane Baukiewicz, who was rather unwell. Having been a former Vicar General of the Community and a directress of Postulants, this seasoned religious woman had witnessed many young women come and go. When asked about Faustina she would say only, "Helen is an interior soul." It is impossible however to know if she knew the full extent of Faustina's interior life, but it seems clear from this comment that she may have been aware something extraordinary was taking place in Faustina's life.

It was not too long after her entry into the convent, and possibly as a result of her change of lifestyle, that Faustina became unwell which was evident in her physical appearance. Other members of the community began to be concerned about her. She looked exhausted and at the suggestion of the Superior was sent for rest to Skolimow, a summer house for the sisters. Accompanying her on the journey were two other members of the community and it became Faustina's assignment to prepare their meals.

The communications with Jesus continued and Faustina began seeking instructions through dialogue with one, whom she believed was Christ Himself. She would ask Jesus during these encounters specifically whom she should pray for. On one occasion Jesus responded that He would give her an answer the following evening. The next night she began to experience what appears to be a journey into Purgatory. When her writings were later analyzed by experts it was concluded that only someone with a great knowledge of theology and mysticism would be capable of such a detailed description unless it was divinely imparted. Ultimately of course the Vatican would believe no other explanation could be possible yet this was of little consolation to Faustina as she tried to convince those around her she was receiving messages from Christ. The attitude of her fellow nuns towards Faustina was quite understandable for though her observations were quite beautiful they certainly had a ring of the fantastical about them. Consider if you will any Mother superior being presented with the following writings by a woman who had hardly any education:

> *[The next night] I saw my Guardian Angel, who ordered me to follow him. In a moment I was in a misty place full of fire in which there was a great crowd of suffering souls. They were praying fervently, but to no avail, for themselves; only we can come to their aid. The flames which were burning them did not touch me at all. My Guardian Angel did not leave me for an instant. I asked these souls what their greatest suffering was. They answered me in one voice that their greatest torment was longing for God. I saw Our Lady visiting the souls in Purgatory. The souls call her "The star of the Sea." She brings them refreshment. I wanted to talk with them some more, but my Guardian Angel beckoned me to leave. We went out of that prison of suffering. [I heard an interior voice] which said, My mercy does not want this but justice demands it. Since that time, I am in closer communion with the suffering souls.*
>
> **—Diary entry 20**

Faustina continued so obediently with all of her assigned tasks that it was difficult for those around her not to see in her a definite commitment to religious life. As a result, after nine months of postulancy, she was able to join the novitiate in Krakow. It was a moment of great personal joy but one also marked by sadness... Upon arrival, one of the Sisters was dying, and a few days later, following her death, Sister Henry, the deceased Sister, according to Faustina, visited her in spirit and asked her go to the Mother Directress, and request the confessor say Mass for her and prayers. While Faustina initially agreed, on second thought, not completely convinced whether it was only a dream or delusion she had experienced she decided not to go. However, according to Faustina as stated in her Diary, Sister Henry returned and Faustina was convinced this was not a dream. As a result she went to the superior and told her everything. The superior assured Faustina that she would take care of the matter and at that moment peace reigned in Faustina's soul. Clearly this humble soul was not concerned about making a fool of herself.

If God was in fact using Faustina for a mission as her subsequent canonization seems to confirm she certainly obeyed him and this trait continued throughout her life often causing great emotional turmoil for her. At the ceremony to receive her habit, God let Faustina know how much she would suffer in religious life. Clothing day was April 30, 1926; exactly eighty four years to the day that Faustina would be declared a Saint in St Peters Square. As Sister Clemens Buczek recalled in her memoirs, she was helping the candidates put on their habits:

I was to dress Helen Kowalska. After she received the habit at the altar I told her, 'Helen, let's hurry to put on your habit.' Helen fainted. I hurried to get the smelling salts in order to revive her... Later I used to tease her about her loathing to leave the world. I only found out after her death that the reason of her fainting was not sorrow for the world but something else.

Indeed Sister Faustina—as she was so named at this veiling, which means fortunate or blessed—had fainted because she received an interior message from God. It was a moment of realization of what lay in store for her, which she later noted in her Diary:

The day I took the [religious] habit, God let me understand how much I was to suffer. I clearly saw to what I was committing myself. I experienced a moment of that suffering. But then God filled my soul again with great consolations.

—Diary entry 22

Over the next few years, Faustina would deepen her spiritual life in meditation and through various devotions. She learned to study the vows of the congregation, the meaning of the vows she would take, and the fundamentals of the Catholic faith. Throughout the novitiate Faustina was on trial, and the superiors were constantly assessing her suitability. It soon became apparent to all that during moments of prayer her behavior showed a greater reverence for the Majesty of God than the other novices did. Faustina's sense of obedience and humility was also very apparent to all those around her.

On one occasion while working in the kitchen and praying out loud with another sister, Faustina realized she had not asked for permission; she immediately went to her superior and asked her permission to pray. On another occasion, her fellow nun, Sister Placida asked in the absence of a superior who would take charge, Faustina conceding, "Sister dear, do not lose Holy peace over such things. Let us work to satisfy Jesus." Clearly Faustina had no desire to be the superior of the Convent and despite her Holiness never became one.

It is interesting to note that these acts of humility were not recorded in her Diary which actually provides confirmation of her humble and contrite disposition. By all accounts Faustina was a joy to be around, and during recreation everyone wanted to be near the young woman and even called her "Our theologian." Moreover, while it seemed on the surface that many were genuinely fond of this fascinating woman, there were many however who often whispered among themselves about her "alleged" conversations with Christ.

For the most part, Faustina put any negativity behind her and seemed to enjoy life. She had a passion for the outdoors; a trait she had developed from childhood and constantly thanked God for the beauty of His creation and acknowledged that everything was from Him.

Towards the end of the first year of her novitiate however darkness began to reign in Faustina's soul. Even prayer, seemed to bring little consolation. Fear swept over her. Realizing the Supreme Holiness of God, Faustina was unable to raise her eyes to Him, and so she mentally reduced herself to dust at His feet and begged for Mercy. Word spread throughout the community that she was experiencing interior struggles but not even attempts

by her Mother directress to encourage her appeared to
help. Clearly Faustina was experiencing a "dark night
of the soul" as witnessed by so many other mystics and
Saints in Church history, particularly John of the Cross
with whom the expression has become synonymous. In
Faustina's case the Diary entries on this matter suggest
she suffered much pain. "From early morning, the
turmoil in my soul was more violent than anything I
had experienced before. Complete abandonment by
God.."

(Diary entry 496)

Feeling utterly rejected by God, Faustina desired to die and she began to experience a deep spiritual agony. It was the reassurance of her Mistress of Novices, that seemed to sustain her;

"Know sister that God has chosen you for great sanctity. This is a sign that God wants to have you very close to Himself in Heaven. Have great trust in the Lord Jesus."

Faustina's work assignments offered no relief. At one point when assigned to the kitchen, Faustina found it difficult to handle the large pots and pans. Even drawing the potatoes became a huge struggle. Exhibiting behavior that was ordinarily out of her character, she even started avoiding work in the kitchen all together. Then suddenly she received these words in her soul. *"From today on in all you will do I shall strengthen you."* From this moment on she was filled with strength. She lifted up the pot, opened the lid and it was full of roses. Standing there astounded by the vision she heard these words. *"I change such hard work of yours into beautiful bouquets of most beautiful flowers, and their perfume rises up to my throne."* From this moment on Faustina was convinced that any assignment given to her was pleasing to God.

Yet the interior struggles did not stop, and as she had no spiritual director to help her, aside from the priest assigned to the convent, this all became a horrific burden. For while Faustina was prepared to accept everything that came her way she still felt totally abandoned. It was at this juncture that she called on a Saint whom she held close to her heart and one whose picture adorned her tiny cell. Faustina petitioned St. Therese of the Child Jesus, to whom she had always had a great devotion. Affectionately known as 'the little flower' and canonized by the Vatican in 1925, today, Therese is a Saint many Catholics believe has special powers. It was during the fifth day of the novena, (a nine day petition of prayers which many Catholics pray) that according to Diary entries she appeared to Faustina in a dream and her words not only gave comfort but also proved to be somewhat prophetic. According to the Diary entry Therese told her; **"Do not be worried about this matter, but trust more in God. I suffered greatly too."** Such was the extent of Faustina's suffering she replied: **"It seems to me that you have not suffered at all."** (Diary entry 150)

Whether or not one can accept such conversations as genuine or not, it is interesting to note that when Faustina asked of her, **"Dear Saint Therese will I go to heaven?"** She answered; **"Yes you will go to heaven Sister."** To which Faustina enquired. **"And will I be a Saint?"**

"Yes you will be a Saint." Therese responded.

"But little Therese, will I be a Saint as you are, named at the altar?"

Therese answered, **"Yes, you will be a Saint just as I am but you must trust in the Lord Jesus."**

We now know that this encounter came true; Faustina did indeed become a Saint. Yet ironically in her lifetime, she would often have a difficult time persuading those around her that she was even sane.

In October 1928, Faustina returned to her old convent in Warsaw and while suffering with her interior suffering, she took consolation in the crucifixion and seemed reconciled to suffer as Christ did without complaint. Adding to her burden however was the realization that her visions and communications had been made known throughout the community, some sisters even insinuated that she was faking her "Illusions"; it was indeed a time of great struggle for her. Well aware of what was transpiring behind her back, Faustina confided to Jesus that she might in fact be a burden to her community. At which point He told her; "You are not living for yourself but for souls, and other souls will profit from your sufferings. Your prolonged suffering will give them light and the strength to accept my will."

One sister who became aware of Faustina's alleged communication chose to point out that God associates in such a way only with Saints and not with sinners like herself. The particular Sister accused Faustina of greatly deluding herself. Faustina went back to Jesus and asked Him; "Are You not an illusion?" He answered; *"My love deceives no one."*

Faustina was becoming increasingly frightened, not even Priests or her superiors seemed able to help her. After all, here she was communicating with Christ Himself. Whom could she tell? It was a period of isolation and confusion. Exacerbating her predicament, one sister who was highly suspicious of her communications told Faustina she could no longer help. "Sister isn't this an illusion of sort? You'd better go and seek the advice of a Priest," Faustina was made aware that all of this was God's doing and this sustained her, but the doubt and suspicion was extremely painful, especially knowing that some of her sisters believed she was possessed.

Despite the doubt that seemed to surround her, Faustina could not turn her back on God on whom she was becoming entirely dependent. He was, it seemed, the only one she could count on for reassurance, at one point telling her; *"You are My heart's delight."* Then Faustina's communion with Christ started to become more specific. Clearly she was being tested. On one occasion Christ instructed Faustina to go to her Superior; *"Go to Mother Superior and ask her to let you wear a hair shirt for seven days, and once each night, you are to get up and come to the chapel."* I said yes, but found a certain difficulty in actually going to the Superior. In the evening Jesus asked me, *"How long will you put it off?"* I made up my mind to tell Mother Superior the very next time I would see her.

As Christ would soon inform her, obedience to His will was clearly being ascertained;

> *"I was here during your conversation with the Superior and know everything, I don't demand mortification from you, but obedience. By obedience you give great glory to Me and gain more for yourself."*

Diary entry 28

As the dialogue continued Faustina was receiving the grace to trust in Him. The conversations were now building up to Faustina's main mission, the assignment that Christ had destined for her; the one she was to share with the whole world.

CHAPTER FOUR

THE IMAGE

"Paint an image according to the pattern you see, with the signature: Jesus, I trust in You. I desire that this image be venerated, first in your chapel, and [then] throughout the world."

—Diary entry 47

In order to fully understand why Faustina was instructed to have an image painted, we should examine how important images have been to civilizations during the course of time. In fact throughout the history of the world and even as far back as the earliest civilizations— imagery, art, and signs have always held a high place of significance for humanity. Confirmation of this reality is provided by the existence of a cave complex on the Nullarbor Plain in Australia that to reach by foot requires a journey of many days from the nearest source of human sustenance. The place consists of a series of chambers that are literally hundreds of feet below the surface of the earth. Despite its remote location however, distinguished Art Curator, Ori Z. Soltes and author of "Our Sacred Signs," reminds us that on the walls of these caves are markings that were made by humans, thousands of years ago. This begs the question: "Why would a group of individuals walk so far and then make their way deep into the earth to systematically decorate the surfaces of that underground world? The most likely explanation is that they were responding to an urge—to be in contact with forces they believed had created them and which also had the power to destroy them, to help or harm them, bless or curse them. And somehow they had come to believe that this particular location was conducive to making contact." These people certainly went beyond the extra mile to find it!

Now, thousands of year's later, people who feel the need to connect with what they believe to be a higher power also reach out and travel long distances. Catholics and Orthodox Christians go on pilgrimages. Jews visit Israel to pray at the Western—or the Wailing Wall. Muslims are expected to fulfill one of the pillars of Islam by visiting Mecca in Saudi Arabia at least once in their lifetime. Many religious practices are very much structured in the same way. Yet, despite their many similarities, with reference to the use of sacred imagery for worship, Christianity stands alone among the monotheistic world religions. Iconography, symbolism, and sacred art have played a vital role from the earliest days of Christianity, and with good reason. Early Christians were often hunted and punished by the Roman government for their religious beliefs and practices. They often had to keep their faith a secret and used signs and pictures often with hidden meanings. A drawing of a fish represented Christ—the dove was the sign of the Holy Spirit—a ship's mast or a ship's anchor was a sign for the cross—and a picture of a meal was used to illustrate the Christian Communion service. All these symbols and pictures were used in the catacombs, during Christianity's greatest periods of persecution. Imagery and symbols were used to keep the faith alive.

Then as Christianity became accepted by the Roman emperors, people felt free to hang pictures on the wall, adorn Crucifixes, and pronounce their faith. However, things were to change when 500 years later a group in the Byzantine Empire, led by the emperor himself, became known as iconoclasts or "icon smashers." They burned icons, hacked down mosaics and painted over anything that could not be broken.

Now at the turn of the twenty-first century we have also witnessed outrage over religious symbols; the Ten Commandments have been removed from court rooms, the words Christmas and Easter have been replaced by "holiday," and more recently we have witnessed controversy and violence over the depiction of the prophet Muhammad in cartoon form in a Danish newspaper. Riots broke out with embassies being attacked and burnt. Violent protests sprung up all over the world. There was even a $million offer by a cleric in Pakistan to anyone who killed one of the cartoonists. The drawings, first printed in Denmark, angered Muslims worldwide and at least 44 people died in protests. The outrage allegedly stemmed from anger because Islamic tradition prohibits any depiction of Allah or Muhammad. Others have said that the whole affair was purposefully staged in order to strike fear into the hearts of any who would attempt to speak negatively about Muhammad or Islam.

This was not the first example of apparent outrage over the depiction of the prophet Muhammad. In Italy in August 2002 Police arrested five people on suspicion of plotting to attack a church in the northern city of Bologna. The men - one Italian and four Moroccans - were reportedly held after being seen filming in and around the city's San Petronio basilica. The arrests follow reports in the Italian media that the al-Qaeda network was planning to bomb the basilica, which contains a fresco considered by some Muslims to be offensive. The 15th Century work depicts the Prophet Muhammad being devoured by demons in Hell.

In another very unusual case, on March 30 2006, Benet Koleka of Reuters news agency reported, "Muslims in Albania's northern city of Shkoder are opposing plans to erect a statue to Mother Teresa, the ethnic Albanian Catholic nun in line for elevation to sainthood by the Vatican." The dispute is unusual for Albania, where religion was banned for 27 years under the regime of Dictator Enver Hoxha, and where religious harmony and mixed marriages are the norm. Seventy percent of the population are liberal Muslims, the rest are Christian Orthodox and Catholic. Yet Muslims in Shkoder had recently protested against the erection of crosses on prominent hilltops in the area and now they rejected the local council plan for a Teresa statue, saying that it "would offend the feelings of Muslims." "We do not want this statue to be erected in a public place," said Bashkim Bajraktari, Shkoder's mufti or Muslim religious leader. All in all, it is a sad reflection on sentiments towards the woman Beatified by the Vatican in October, 2003 who once described herself this way: "By blood, I am Albanian, by citizenship, an Indian, by faith a Catholic nun. As to my calling, I belong to the world."

More recently in a move closer to home on October 10, 2006, an Islamist website posted a message alerting Muslims to what it claims is a new insult to Islam. According to the message, the cube-shaped building which has just been constructed in New York City, on Fifth Avenue between 58th and 59th Streets in midtown Manhattan, is clearly meant to provoke Muslims. The fact that the building resembles the Ka'ba is called "Apple Mecca," and is intended to be open 24 hours a day like the Ka'ba, and moreover, contains bars selling alcoholic beverages, constitutes a blatant insult to Islam." The message urged Muslims to spread this alert, in hope that "Muslims will be able to stop the project." They were not able to but clearly an 'Apple' symbol, the logo of Mac computers in a city nicknamed the 'Big Apple' seems to be extending political correctness to the extreme, and is certainly a far cry from the messages that were given to Faustina! The messages contained in the Diary are of love, inclusion, and hope for a troubled world.

Clearly for centuries religious imagery and symbolism has caused—or staved—tidal waves throughout the history of humanity. Yet in the history of images and symbols there is not one that shares the same significance as *The Divine Mercy Image*: A painting commissioned by Christ to prepare the world for His final coming.

It was the evening of February 22, 1931, when alone in her cell, Faustina claimed to have seen Jesus. Outside of the convent walls this vision came at a time when there was much conflict in the world. It was a year when the faint rumblings of war were already being heard over the horizon. Japan had taken over Manchuria, which would be renamed Manchukuo. Though Adolph Hitler was beginning his rise to prominence in Germany, no one could have known that in a few short years, seemingly the whole world would be plunged into war.

Why Faustina would have been given visions at this historical juncture certainly seems to fit in with prophecy. Traditionally through the history of God's dealings with mankind—certainly throughout the Bible and in Church history, He has always sent various messages to people, often to inform them of a grand mission that would alter the course of the world—or a part of the world. Many people believe that a Bible prophecy is a God-given revelation of the future. God gave His prophets messages to prepare people for the future, and to show that He is the one true God and is all-powerful. A prophecy, according to many believers, is not a prediction of the future - it is a promise about the future.

Beginning with Moses and carrying on through both the Old and New Testaments, prophets and apostles have received the word of God. Even in our lifetime, holy people like Mother Teresa have been asked to listen to God's word and follow His promptings. Often the assignments seemed impossible for the person but in keeping with the will of God, they managed in miraculous fashion to fulfill them. Faustina was also called to such a task. As Jesus told her:

> *"In the Old Covenant—I sent prophets wielding thunderbolts to My people. Today I am sending you with My mercy to the people of the whole world. I do not want to punish aching mankind, but I desire to heal it, pressing it to My Merciful Heart.*

> **— Diary entry 1588**

In light of messages like this one, Pope John Paul II was ultimately prompted to proclaim Saint Faustina "the great apostle of Divine Mercy in our time." It was a sentiment echoed by her biographer Sister Sophia Michaelenko who says: "We can truly think of Saint Faustina as the Prophet Jeremiah, who said: 'The word of the Lord came to me, saying, 'Before I formed you in the womb I knew you, before you were born I set you apart; I appointed you as prophet to the nations'" (Jer 1:4-5). Yet the prophet recoiled at the awesomeness of the task, saying, "Ah, Sovereign Lord, I do not know how to speak; I am only a child" (v.6). To which the Lord replied, "Do not say, 'I am only a child.' You must go to everyone I send you to and say whatever I command you. Do not be afraid of them, for I am with you and will rescue you" (VV.7-8). As Sister Sophia concludes, "If we are to believe the revelations Faustina received as true, which her Canonization seems to warrant, we must also see this humble servant of God as one who is destined by God's mercy and designed to play a most special role in the history of the Church. Consider for example, these predictions to her made by Jesus as well as The Virgin Mary on several occasions. Christ told her: *"You will prepare the world for My final coming"* — **Diary entry 429.** And from The Virgin Mary:

> *"I gave the Savior of the world, as for you, you have to speak to the world about His great mercy and prepare the world for the second coming of Him who will come, not as a merciful Savior, but as a just judge"*

> **—Diary entry 635**

With such a task entrusted to her it is hard to imagine what would have gone through Faustina's mind when she claimed she actually saw Jesus standing before her clothed in a white garment. As she described the moment in her Diary, one of His hands was raised in the gesture of blessing; the other was touching the garment at the breast. Beneath the garment were radiating two large rays, one red, the other pale. In silence she kept her eyes fixed on Him. Though obviously shocked, her writings of this encounter mention nothing of fear.

It was moments after His visit that He gave her the message that would forever change her life and the life of Pope John Paul II.

> *"Paint an image according to the pattern you see, with the signature: Jesus, I trust in You. I desire that the image be venerated, first in your chapel, and [then] throughout the world. I promise that the soul that will venerate this image will not perish. I promise victory over [its] enemies already here on earth, especially at the hour of death. I Myself will defend it as My own glory."*
>
> — **Diary entry 49**

Such an encounter is clearly not something most people would believe, and when Faustina discussed the matter with her priest, he told her that it was not to be taken literally but it was an instruction to paint the image in her soul. Again Faustina claimed to receive more words from Christ.

> *My image is already in your soul. I desire that there be a Feast of Mercy. I want this image, which you will paint with a brush, to be solemnly blessed on the first Sunday after Easter; that Sunday is to be the Feast of Mercy."* **Christ continued,** *"I desire that priests proclaim this great mercy of Mine towards the souls of sinners. Let the sinner not be afraid to approach Me. The flames of mercy are burning Me—clamoring to be spent; I want to pour them out upon these souls.*
>
> —**Diary entry 50**

According to Faustina's account of the moment, Christ then complained to her in these words,

> *Distrust on the part of souls is tearing at My insides. The distrust of a chosen soul causes Me even greater pain; despite My inexhaustible love for them, they do not trust Me. Even My death is not enough for them. Woe to the soul that abuses these [gifts].*

—**Diary entry 50**

Even though other holy men and women have had apparitions, Faustina's superior was not completely convinced that this was the case. After all what would one do if told Jesus visited a convent and only one nun actually saw Him? As a result Mother Rose was somewhat skeptical and told Faustina that if indeed this were all God's will, then Jesus would provide some sign to recognize Him. When Faustina went back to Christ and asked Him for further confirmation, she heard this interior voice.

> *"I will make this clear to the Superior by means of the graces which I will grant through this image."*

Diary entry 51

This would not be the first time that a painting would play a significant role in the history of Poland. One possible reason as to why Poland was chosen for this mission might be explained through the country's historic trust and belief in images.

For centuries the miraculous Icon of Our Lady of Czestochowa (the Black Madonna) has remained in Poland. It is one of the oldest Icons in the world. Both Faustina and Pope John Paul II loved to visit the Jasna Gora Sanctuary in Czestochowa. This site is also mentioned in her diary. Jasna Gora is considered by Poles to be one of the holiest places in Poland and has long been one of the world's most important destinations for pilgrims in Europe. The Jasna Gora (Bright Mount) sanctuary in Czestochowa, is a ninety minutes' drive northwest from Krakow, and has been Central Europe's spiritual hub for six centuries.

Europeans are also very much aware that they owe an enormous sense of gratitude to Poland because it was at Vienna on September 11th 1683, that the Polish King would defeat the Ottoman Empire and allow

Christainity to reign in Europe. As a result every year several million pilgrims—commoners as well as celebrities—visit Poland's national shrine and pray before the miraculous picture of Our Lady of Czestochowa. The faithful have believed for centuries that St. Luke the Evangelist himself painted the divine icon on a tabletop from the Holy Family's house in Nazareth in 328 A.D.; the family home of Jesus Christ. As legend follows St Helena then found the Icon in Jerusalem and brought it to Constantinople where it remained until it was taken to Poland. Many in Poland have entrusted the future of their country and the world through prayer to this painting.

In 1430 a band of Hussite marauders ransacked the Jasna Gora treasury and carried off the picture of Our Lady. According to legend, when the band neared St. Barbara's Church, the frightened horses refused to go any further. In a blind rage, one of the band threw the picture out of the carriage and slashed it with his sword. Then all fled. Sometime later, a group of Pauline Fathers found the damaged picture and washed it in a spring that miraculously appeared in the area of the church. To this day the faithful consider the spring waters miraculous. Informed about the damage to the picture, King Ladislaus Jagiello personally arranged to have it restored. He imported expert artists, who executed the restoration with admirable skill. Traces of the sword cuts are still visible on the Virgin Mary's face as a constant reminder of the desecration. In 1621 during the reign of Zygmunt III, Karl Chodkiewicz became the general of the Polish armed forces fighting against the Turks. Chodkiewicz was a chivalrous soldier with great love and veneration for the Virgin of Czestochowa. During the Turkish siege of Chocim, Chodkiewicz ordered the outnumbered Polish troops to pray fervently to Our Lady of Czestochowa for help. He knew that by restraining the westward march of the Turks, Poland would be defending Catholic Europe against the flood of Islamism. He could be confident then, that Mary would aid this noble venture.

On October 10, when after a month's siege, the Polish camp was left with only one barrel of ammunition; Chodkiewicz began to question the possibility of further defense. Inspired, however, by a renewed confidence in the Virgin Mary, he decided to continue the battle and ordered the Polish soldiers to intensify their prayers. On that very day, October 10th, the Turks were dealt such a severe blow that they pleaded for peace terms. It was later learned that at that very time, Fr. Oborski, a Jesuit, had had a vision at prayer. He saw St. Stanislaus Kostka begging The Virgin Mary for the grace of victory for the Poles, and his prayer was heard. In thanksgiving for the end of the war, General Chodkiewicz and King Ladislaus IV publicly attributed this remarkable victory against the Turks to Our Lady of Czestochowa. In more recent times, Poland has also witnessed the influence of Our Lady of Czestochowa. In 1956, as the country was undergoing a time of growing tension between the government and the Church due to Soviet dominance, it was before this image the people prayed. The Cardinal Primate Wyszynski was under house arrest for three years, and many others were jailed. Then from Jasna Gora came an inspiration to the Cardinal: Mary will hasten with help as she did 300 years ago.

On August 26, the feast of Our Lady of Czestochowa, a crowd of a million faithful besieged Jasna Gora. This time it was a siege of prayer, sacrifice, and repentance and John Casimir's Vows which declared the Mother of God to be the Queen of Poland were renewed. The Nation promised fidelity to its Mother and Queen and begged for freedom for the Cardinal Primate and for the Church in Poland. The country waited for two months, and then on the last Saturday of October, Cardinal Wyszynski was allowed to return to Warsaw to resume his duties. Thanking the people of Poland for their prayers, he said: "I prayed in prison that if I should be freed that it should happen through the Mother of God, and as a sign of this victory that it may happen on her day and in her month. And it happened thus."

Pope Pius XI, who had been the Apostolic Nuncio to Poland in 1918, kept a copy of Our Lady of Czestochowa in the Vatican chapel during his tenure as Pope. During World War I British air force pilots kept the image in a hangar of their bomber squadron. Today there is also a copy of the painting hanging prominently at St Patrick's Cathedral in New York. Clearly the legend of this image's miraculous powers has reached far and wide.

Now years later this image is still being referenced. In September 2006, just days after the furor of comments made by Pope Benedict XVI regarding a Byzantine Emperor's words on Islam, Italian Journalist and bestselling author Oriana Fallaci passed away. In her book, *The Force of Reason*, she spoke of the image of the Black Madonna. Fallaci, who had spent a lifetime telling the truth, had, since attacks of September 11th, written about fundamentalist Islam's threat to western culture and to Christianity in Europe. Though some of her language may have been derogatory, clearly there was no political or theological agenda. Fallaci simply saw how Europe was changing and wrote about it. A self-proclaimed atheist who had resisted fascism, Fallaci's concern was her fear of theocracy and dictatorship from which she had escaped as a child. In fact, after 9/11 Fallaci who had made her home in New York was genuinely concerned about the world's future and particularly Europe, where Christianity was rapidly disappearing. She had even met with Pope Benedict to voice her concerns. Sadly, for her honesty she was accused of defaming Islam and went to her death awaiting trial, but her words live on. When referring to Our Lady of Czestochowa she said in *The Force of Reason*:

Remember what John Sobieski, the heroic king of Poland, shouted to his soldiers during the battle that in 1683 repelled Kara Mustafa? He shouted: Soldiers, it is not Vienna alone that we must save! It is Christianity, the same idea of Christendom! And remember what he added soon after? He added Soldiers! Let's fight for Our Lady of Czestochowa.

That's right; *Our Lady of Czestochowa*. Clearly the legend of this image has reached many circles. And so even as the Image of Our Lady of Czestochowa was instrumental in the curtailing of attacks against western civilization on various occasions, so now, once again, as the threat is renewed, the world has been given another Image. Again this one also finds its origins in the country of Poland and is also fully endorsed by the Vatican: *The Image of Divine Mercy*. Is this all part of the Divine plan?

Certainly in the history of Christianity images seem to have played a significant role. In Mexico where the Aztecs worshipped an evil stone "serpent god" that demanded human sacrifice, the Virgin Mary appeared to a humble Aztec Indian convert by the name of Juan Diego in 1531. When asked her name by Juan Diego, at the request of the local bishop, Our Lady's response, in the Aztec language, included the words "te coatlaxopeuh" (pronounced: "te quatlasupe") and meant "one who crushes the head of the stone serpent." Today she is known as Our Lady of Guadalupe but to Juan Diego and his fellow Aztecs, this revelation had great meaning, coupled with the miraculous image of Our Lady standing on top of a crescent moon—the symbol of this evil serpent god. A tidal wave of conversions to Catholicism ensued. However, Bishop Zumarraga, who was from Spain, made what was no doubt a "heavenly mistake" to the Bishop's

Spanish ears, Our Lady's Aztec name of "Te Quatlasupe" sounded just like the name of the revered Madonna from Spain with the Arabic name, "Guadalupe." Hence, the bishop named the Mexican Madonna "Our Lady of Guadalupe." It is interesting that on one hand, the "crescent" is also the symbol for Islam and that America's Shrine to Our Lady has an Arabic name.

Miraculously the image of Our Lady of Guadalupe would be used fifty years after Juan Diego's vision on October 7, 1571 thousands of miles away in Spain. It was at the battle of LePanto, where a great victory over the mighty Turkish fleet was won by Catholic naval forces primarily from Spain, Venice, and Genoa under the command of Don Juan of Austria. It was the last battle at sea between "oared" ships, which featured the most powerful navy in the world, a Muslim force with between 12,000 to 15,000 Christian slaves as rowers. One of three admirals commanding the Catholic forces at Lepanto was Andrea Doria. He carried a small copy of Mexico's Our Lady of Guadalupe into battle and as the enemy approached, the image was taken to the helm of the ship.

Meanwhile back on land and aware that the Christian forces were at a distinct material disadvantage, Pope Pius V called for all of Europe to pray the Rosary for victory. The victory was decisive, and prevented the Islamic invasion of Europe. In fact, at the hour of victory, Pope Pius V, is said to have gotten up from a meeting, at the Vatican, walked over to a window, and exclaimed with supernatural radiance: "The Christian fleet is victorious!" and shed tears of thanksgiving to God.

Today the original of this image, is now enshrined in the Church of San Stefano in Aveto, Italy. While at the Monastery of Our Lady of Guadalupe in Spain, one can view a huge warship lantern that was captured from the Muslims in the Battle of Lepanto. In 1965, an Islamic flag from the battle was returned to Istanbul in a friendly token of concord having previously been on display at Saint Mary Major Basilica in Rome, close to the tomb of the great Pope Pius V.

The Vatican believes the victory at Lepanto was won by the faithful praying the Rosary and the presence of Our Lady of Guadalupe's image. As a result, the Battle of Lepanto was celebrated liturgically as "Our Lady of Victory." The feast of October 7th was later renamed "Our Lady of the Rosary" and extended throughout the Universal Church by Pope Clement XI in 1716 (who canonized Pope Pius V in 1712).

It is evident that long before Faustina's vision, images and icons have been successful vessels in saving the Church. Yet Faustina could not have known how her particular instruction might be of relevance in the next century. Consequently not realizing the implications of her mission and what significance this image might hold for the 21st century, back in the 1930's Faustina found the assigned task impossible and tried to run away from her visions. It appears that Divine providence would have the last word. For as hard as she tried, she could not run from this calling. Tortured by the enormity of this task, Faustina went to her confessor at the convent and asked to be dispensed from getting this Image painted. Nevertheless, Father Andrasz, who would become one of her most trusted friends, would not do it. "I will dispense you from nothing, Sister, it is not right for you to turn away from these interior inspirations, but you must absolutely speak about them to your confessor; otherwise you will go astray despite the graces you are receiving from God." The priest was adamant that she also find a permanent spiritual director. Once again, Faustina was at a loss; she felt she could not talk about these things to a confessor. She begged Jesus to assign the task to someone else because the graces were wasted on her. "Jesus have mercy on me; do not entrust such great things to me, as You see that I am a bit of dust and completely inept," she prayed. However, having promised her visible help, she was to receive a vision in the form of a priest named Father Sopocko and she heard the voice of God,

"This is the visible help for you on earth. He will help you carry out My will on earth."

Diary entry 53

Again plagued by torment as she found herself doubted and discouraged by her superiors, Faustina asked Jesus in prayer whether these were illusions or phantoms she was seeing. She begged forgiveness at having asked the question but was reassured that her confidence was very pleasing to Him. These sentiments would be reassured during spiritual consultation, when she was once again told by Father Andrasz not to turn away from these inspirations.

Deeper and deeper became her trust in God even though the visions drew her further apart from everybody else. It was necessary for Faustina to learn to completely detach from this world and trust entirely on the next. Yet the whisperings of her fellow sisters who had come to know of her connection with God did reach her ears and she was worried about being a burden to her community. On one occasion, one of the mothers yelled at her in front of the other sisters, "You queer, hysterical visionary, get out of this room; go on with you Sister!" Again, she was reassured by Jesus, *"You are not living for yourself but for souls, and other souls will profit from your sufferings. Your prolonged suffering will give them light and strength to accept My will."* (Diary entry 67)

There was still the matter of the painting: She couldn't paint and she did not know what to do. One of the sisters told her that someone had said she was a fantasist and that she should defend herself. Again Faustina turned to God, who told her, *"Be at peace My daughter, it is precisely through such misery that I want to show the power of My mercy."* (Diary entry 133) However, there was no relief from the matter of the painting, and she received warning of the grave consequences that would follow if she failed in her mission. *"know that if you neglect the matter of the painting of the Image and the whole work of mercy, you will have to answer for a multitude of souls on the judgment day."* (Diary entry 154) Consumed with fear and alarmed, she went to the chapel, fell on her face, and begged for God to remain at her side.

As her visions continued and the conversations appeared to became more frequent, Faustina continued to discuss the image with her confessor. With increasing urgency she repeated her conversations with Jesus about the Image and though somewhat skeptical, Father Sopocko, after subjecting Faustina to full psychiatric testing, commissioned Eugene Kazimierowski, a neighborhood artist, to paint what Faustina had described. The priest also asked her to talk to Jesus about the meaning of the rays on the Image. Ever obedient, Faustina did so and received this reply:

> *The two rays denote Blood and Water. The pale ray stands for the water, which makes souls righteous. The red ray stands for the blood which is the life of souls.... These two rays issued forth from the very depths of My tender Mercy when My agonized Heart was opened by a lance on the Cross. These rays shield souls from the wrath of My Father. Happy is the one who will dwell in their shelter, for the just hand of God shall not lay hold of him. I desire the first Sunday after Easter be the Feast*

of Mercy. Ask of My faithful servant [Father Sopocko] that on this day, he tells the whole world of My great Mercy; that whoever approaches the Fount of Life on this day will be granted complete remission of sins and punishment. Mankind will not have peace until it turns with trust to My Mercy.

—Diary entry 299

While the artist continued to capture the Image based on Faustina's descriptions, she began to worry that it was not as beautiful as she had seen Jesus in her vision. Faustina went to the chapel and asked "Who will paint You as beautiful as you are?" Then she heard these words: *"Not in the beauty of the color, nor of the brush lies the greatness of this image, but in my grace."* (**Diary entry 313**)

Still overwhelmed by her task, Faustina asked the Mother of God to grant her the ability to live by the power of God. She then received a visitation from Mary who spoke the words: *"You are going to experience certain sufferings because of an illness and the doctors. You will also suffer much because of the Image, but do not be afraid."* **Diary entry 316.** The next day Faustina fell ill.

On another occasion Faustina got so close to death because of her weak lungs that she actually felt the suffering of death, but she received assurance that this was not her time:

My will has not yet been fully accomplished in you. You will still remain on earth, but not for long. I am well pleased with your trust, but your love should be more ardent. Pure love gives the soul strength at the very moment of dying. When I was dying on the cross, I was not thinking about Myself, but about poor sinners, and I prayed for them to My Father. I want your last moments to be completely similar to Mine on the cross.

—**Diary entry 324**

As the artist continued painting the image, Faustina was still not convinced it was right. In fact, it was not until after ten separate attempts that Jesus assured her to let the painting remain as it was. Then came the instruction. *"I desire that the Image be publicly honored."* Now Faustina would find herself confronted with a whole new set of obstacles when she discussed the matter with her priest, he told her it would be impossible. In fact Father Spocko told her that the notion of introducing a feast on the Sunday after Easter was not something of which he could even conceive. Divine intervention would again prevail and when soon thereafter, he learned that he would be delivering a sermon on that day he then agreed to allow the Image to be displayed in the Church for three days before he spoke.

Two other artists, namely Stanley Batowski and Adolf Hyla would also be asked to paint the Image. Hyla was commissioned following Faustina's death and the work was finished in 1943. With three images there was now the issue of which one would hang in the sister's chapel, and because Hyla's work was done by the artist as a votive offering it was this Divine Mercy image that was placed in the chapel of Faustina's convent.

Meanwhile during her lifetime many judgments were being cast against Faustina's character at this time. Sisters from within her own religious order were extremely skeptical not only about her claims of the messages but also her motives. First Faustina claimed to receive direct communications from and visions of Christ, then she said she received instructions to have a painting commissioned which was based on one of her visions, and now she was even requesting that the Image would be venerated and recognized publicly on the Sunday after Easter. Many thought her to be full of delusions of grandeur.

Yet Divine providence was evidently at her side. Jesus reassured her of His delight in her obedience, **"You are a witness to My mercy. You shall stand before My throne forever as a living witness to My mercy." (Diary entry 417)**

Her task seemed complete. Faustina may have thought she could rest, but she would soon come to understand her task was far from complete. Commissioning the Image was just the beginning. Now as Jesus had instructed, the image still had to be shown throughout the world—to prepare the world for His final coming!

CHAPTER FIVE

A TRUSTING SOUL

"Why are you afraid? Do you think that I will not have enough omnipotence to support you?"

—Diary entry 527

After Faustina received her first vision of Christ and was given instructions to have the Divine Mercy Image painted, one would expect that if these directions were truly of divine origin, that she would have been given a confirming degree of divine support. After all, if all this were really the work of God, then wouldn't He make things easy? Would not God Himself have put the right people in place quickly so that the painting would be produced and distributed throughout the world? Would not God Himself have seen to it that the Vatican would subsequently sanction the prayer that Faustina was given to accompany the image promptly? Yet things would not transpire this way at all. Instead, Faustina was required to rely solely on faith and remain obedient to that which she clearly believed was God's will. For in the same manner that God has acted with all of the other Saints throughout history, He did not make this assignment easy for Faustina. Instead the whole process of executing this matter would cause her great heartache and at times it would seem impossible. As a result, Faustina would not only encounter great difficulty throughout her natural life, but from the onset of her first supernatural encounters, she was met with great skepticism from so many around her. So great was the level of suspicion surrounding her, that even her confessor—in whom she confided in accord with Christ's commands regarding the Image—initially discouraged her away from carrying out God's plan.

Today the convent where Faustina received her first instruction is a virtual shrine to this devoted messenger of Christ. Flowers adorn the window box of the room where she saw Christ, and any passerby is well aware that this was the place where Faustina once lived. A short way away from Faustina's former cell is a very large Church built at the instruction of Pope John Paul II in honor of Faustina and the Image of Divine Mercy. Only twenty minutes from the airport in Krakow, thousands of pilgrims visit the center each year. In light of the often torturous rejection that this dear woman endured in this place, it must be seen as a divinely ironic twist that today, Faustina and the Divine Mercy Image are the main attractions at her former convent. For while she received great consolation through her communications with Christ, this would all be a matter of constant heartache for Faustina which she wrote painstakingly about in her diary:

> *All these things could still be endured. But when the Lord demanded that I should paint that picture, they began to speak openly about me and regard me as an hysteric and a fantasist, and rumors began to grow louder.*

> —Diary entry 128

Clearly Faustina's mission was not an easy one and she was well aware that the only one she could ultimately count on was God. In many ways this was what God was asking of the world but the price Faustina was asked to pay was very high.

> *I could now see that everywhere I was being watched like a thief: in the chapel: while I was carrying out my duties; in my cell. I was well aware that, besides the presence of God, I had always close to me a human presence as well*

> —Diary entry 128

In fact, the whole ordeal proved quite troublesome for her. As she recalled;

> *There were times when I wondered whether I should undress to wash myself or not. Indeed, even that poor bed of mine was checked many times. More than once I was seized with laughter when they would not leave my bed alone. One of the sisters herself told me that she came to observe me in my cell every evening to see how I behave in it.*

—Diary entry 128

Yet while the scrutiny she was to endure was intense, this Saint in the making would stick to her seemingly impossible task in much the same way as all of God's messengers have throughout history. From Noah to Moses, from Jeremiah to Obadiah, from the Disciples to the early Saints of the Church, so many of God's messengers endured great suffering but remained obedient to God's call on their lives. Faustina also maintained her trust in God, believing that she was experiencing a significant and unique encounter with Him.

It was a resolve that appeared to pay off, in June of 1934, when the painting was finally finished. Three years later an ecclesiastical commission approved the picture and permitted it to be blessed and displayed for veneration. It finally seemed Faustina had achieved God's will. However, this was only the beginning.

Faustina would then be entrusted with the mission of installing a prayer to accompany the Image. It was an instruction she once again dutifully wrote in her Diary.

> *Every time you enter the chapel, immediately recite the prayer which I taught you yesterday. This prayer will serve to appease My wrath. You will recite it for nine days, on the beads of the rosary, in the following manner: First of all, you will say one Our Father and Hail Mary and the I believe in God. Then on the Our Father beads you will say the following words: "Eternal Father, I offer you the body and blood, soul and Divinity of your dearly beloved son, Our Lord Jesus Christ, in atonement for our*

sins and those of the whole world." **On the Hail Mary beads you will say the following: "For the sake of His sorrowful Passion have mercy on us and on the whole world." In conclusion, three times you will recite these words: " Holy God, Holy Mighty One, Holy Immortal One, have mercy on us and on the whole world.**

—Diary entry 476

Yet while God was imparting these messages with relative frequency the execution of them would prove problematic. Soon the Image, which Faustina had painstakingly described to the artists, would be removed from all Churches, devotion to Divine Mercy curtailed, and Faustina's name no longer mentioned. For while the Image of Divine Mercy was briefly shown in 1935, following Faustina's untimely death in 1938, it was hidden away —along with any recognition of Faustina's role in the matter. For although a small booklet written by Faustina's confessor, Fr. Michael Sopocko, containing various prayers to The Divine Mercy was given an imprimatur—an official sanction by the Church—it never once mentioned Faustina by name. Not that this would have mattered to Faustina personally, for in a world where people are often desperate for attention, Faustina was happy to serve behind the scenes, content it seemed to attend to the Glory of God and fulfill the mission entrusted to her. She knew that trust was the key to her task being executed and though she believed that Jesus commissioned the work, He also allowed her to encounter a number of road blocks. The purpose for this was to show that the work was His and that its fruition would only come to pass in His own time—without Faustina being able to claim any credit. After all, if God gives a person an assignment and they are able to accomplish it quickly, then the person may be tempted to think that they did it themselves. Faustina was never allowed to imagine such a thing. Instead, Faustina appeared to have been assigned a thankless task and one that was met with suspicion and persecution. Yet, retrospectively we can see how God's hand was guiding things from the beginning, and how He continued to guide this work through Pope John Paul II—as well as through various world events—in order to spread this message and devotion.

What sustained Faustina throughout her life were the words of reassurance that she heard from Christ. These communications were consistently accompanied with feelings of such comfort and peace that she never questioned their origin. As she once noted,

> *Jesus filled me with such great peace that, later on, even when I tried to become uneasy, I could not do so. And then I heard these words in my soul: "In order that you may be assured that it is I who am demanding all these things of you, I will give you such profound peace that even if you wanted to feel troubled and frightened, it would not be in your power to do so today, but love will flood your soul to the point of self-oblivion."*

While Faustina's efforts on earth seemed to yield little reward, her direct conversations with Christ and His reassurances kept her going. It wasn't just a mental battle that Faustina would be asked to fight. Soon her failing bought a new set of struggles. Yet in an apparent resolve to attend to her divine duty, Faustina carried on and nothing it seemed could stop her.

CHAPTER SIX

THE MESSAGES CONTINUE

"He will help you carry out My will on earth."

—Diary entry 53

It is hard to imagine how Faustina maintained her strength when dealing with the task entrusted to her. It seems it was only through a combination of her strong faith and assurances from the contents of the messages she was receiving, that she was able to endure. After all, as a nun, she was betrothed to Christ, and the words she believed He was imparting to her were clearly of a very special nature. Also contained in the dialogue were profound and intimate Messages of love and comfort to accompany her on her mission:

> *My child, life on earth is a struggle indeed; a great struggle for My Kingdom. But fear not, because you are not alone. I am always supporting you, so lean on Me as you struggle fearing nothing. Take the vessel of trust and draw from the fountain of life – for yourself, but also for other souls, especially such as are distrustful of My goodness.*

—Diary entry1488

It was quite evident that overriding these messages of love were also strict and very specific instructions intended for mankind:

> *Secretary of My most profound mystery, know that yours is an exclusive intimacy with Me. Your task is to write down everything that I make known to you about My mercy, for the benefit of those who by reading these things will be comforted in their souls and will have the courage to approach Me. I therefore want you to devote all your moments to writing.*

—Diary entry 1693

It is easy to see how with such an interior dialogue taking place Faustina was beginning to feel somewhat isolated from other members of the community. This was a reality Christ made mention of in The Diary; *"Even among the sisters you will feel lonely. Know then that I want to unite yourself more closely to Me. I am concerned about every beat of your heart."* (Diary entry 1542). Ironically, the girls who came off the streets to live at the convent to transform their lives were the first to recognize her holiness. Nevertheless, Faustina's fellow sisters seemingly failed to acknowledge any of the special spiritual gifts this bride of Christ may have been blessed with and certainly did not want to believe she was receiving direct messages.

Sadly, some of her fellow nuns even thought Faustina was no more than a good-for-nothing fantasist and their treatment of her was indicative of the low opinion they had. Indeed, many of the other sisters considered her an uneducated member of the community who suffered strange and possibly demonic illusions. This would add to the burden Faustina felt accompanied her task. Surprisingly though, despite her often poor treatment at the hands of the sisters during her lifetime, after her death, they gave very glowingly positive depositions in order to contribute to her becoming a Saint. Several finally admitted that they loved being near her and that she was indeed a very special soul. Sadly, Faustina was never given this impression while she was alive thus providing proof that she did indeed have the patience of a Saint!

Understandably, the negative reactions Faustina would experience from her community would cause her great heartache. Frequently she struggled with her mission and the messages imparted to her. Yet Divine providence would provide Faustina with Father Michael Sopocko who would help make her task easier. Sopocko's Priestly life was relatively quiet, until he was introduced to Faustina. Fr Sopocko was appointed confessor to The Sisters of Our Lady of Mercy in 1933, and as a result became her confessor. It was an unlikely and surprising confession from Faustina, a simple, yet pious nun when she told Father Sopocko Christ was imparting messages to her. The difficulty in accepting this humble sister's claims was due to the fact that no one believed her testimony. Yet she had prayed for someone to come along who would listen and help her, and it appeared Father Sopocko was the man that was entrusted with this task. As a result, he would become a very dear soul to this most-often misunderstood mystic.

It is difficult to imagine the scene from on the other side of the confessional window, when Faustina started to recount her numerous conversations with Christ. It is still unclear what prompted Father Sopocko to take her seriously but he did. Like Faustina, he also would suffer ridicule for spreading the devotion of Divine Mercy. Yet just following his death he too would be exonerated.

In 2005, the Vatican Congregation for Sainthood Causes recognized the heroic virtues of this man and a miracle attributed to his intercession. As a result Fr. Sopocko was beatified, the first stage towards becoming a Saint. Back in the 1930's however he was an obedient and patient priest who listened attentively as Faustina's messages continued to be relayed. It seemed as though following each message—an experience that would often fill Faustina with a divinely imparted euphoria. Then, however, she would often find herself confronted with despair. Faustina would confide her feelings to Fr. Sopocko who encouraged her to take heart, persevere, and strengthen her faith. Likewise, Jesus Himself would provide her with a deep consolation:

> *My child you please Me most by suffering. In your physical as well as your mental sufferings, My daughter do not seek comfort from creatures. I want the fragrance of your sufferings to be pure and unaltered.*
>
> **—Diary entry 279**

Christ would soon allow Faustina to receive full comprehension of the significance of *The Image* by outlining the importance of the inscription at the bottom of *The Image*, and what the significance of *The Image* really is. *"I am offering people a vessel with which they are to keep coming for graces to the fountain of mercy. That vessel is this image with the signature. "Jesus, I trust in You."* - Diary entry 327

In part three of this book, we will examine a possible reason why humanity might need a vessel, an image of Christ at some point in the future and why the world may also need a specific prayer. Certainly, Jesus allowed Faustina to realize how important to Him this assignment was. In addition, the more aware that Faustina became of God's great plans for her the more it terrified her. Understandably she often felt quite incapable of executing the mission given to her. Such was her reticence that Faustina even started to fear receiving more messages. She tried to read books to avoid further communication. It was at this juncture that she was to receive her most important directive; *"You will prepare the world for My final coming."* -Diary entry 429

The enormity of such a task overwhelmed Faustina as she heard these words in the chapel. Her first instinct was to leave but when she tried she encountered another message;

> *You intend to leave the chapel, but you shall not get away from Me, for I am everywhere. You cannot do anything of yourself, but with Me you can do all things.*
>
> **-Diary entry 429**

While it is easy to become skeptical when hearing of super- natural encounters it is important to note here that Faustina had already undergone—and handily cleared—a stringent mental health evaluation. It was in light of this fact as well as Faustina's humble demeanor that she gained such credibility with her Priest. In fact, when Faustina discussed her fears with Father Sopocko, he told her not to avoid these instructions but to listen attentively. Fearful that she may have offended God in shrugging off her assignment she begged for forgiveness and received yet further messages:

> *My daughter, have fear of nothing; I am always with you. All your adversaries will harm you only to the degree that I permit them to do so. You are my dwelling place*

*and My constant repose. For your sake I will withhold
the hand which punishes; for your sake I will bless the
earth.*

—Diary entry 1011

Faustina, though consoled by such comforting words, was also contemplating whether she should leave her congregation to start another. For it seemed that where she had been placed was not conducive to carrying out God's plan. Yet, through prayer Faustina was led to believe that this was not what God was asking from her, and so she continued to listen attentively to Him.

Soon Faustina would receive messages that suggested that perhaps God wanted her to start another congregation. Her only source of assurance—her faithful priest and a Divine dialogue.

*By your entreaties, you and your companions shall
obtain mercy for yourselves and for the world.*

—Diary entry 435

What was most evident from these messages was the theme of *The Image*, the preparation for Christ's return and the reciting of the Prayer to accompany *The Image*.

*Say unceasingly the chaplet that I have taught you.
Whoever will recite it will receive great mercy at the
hour of death. Priests will recommend it to sinners as
their last hope of salvation. Even if there were a sinner
most hardened, if he were to recite this chaplet only once,
he would receive grace from my infinite mercy. I desire
that the whole world know My infinite mercy. I desire
to grant unimaginable graces to those souls who trust in
My mercy.*

—Diary entry 687

*It was one thing for God to teach Faustina a special
prayer, but it was quite another to expect her to introduce
it to the Church Universal. With the initial help of
Father Sopocko, and ultimately with Pope John Paul II*

as her champion, divine providence would clearly prevail. However, in the meantime, Faustina was wrestling with the world. In private however, Father Sopocko was slowly gaining insight as to what God thought of the world and the Church that represented Him. In fact on one occasion the messages contained a bitter rebuke towards some members of the Catholic Church. " I will allow convents and churches to be destroyed.

- **Diary entry 1702**

To which Faustina probably in a state of astonishment answered, **"Jesus, but there are so many souls praising you in convents."** According to *The Diary*, Jesus answered:

That praise wounds My Heart, because love has been banished from convents. Souls without love and without devotion, souls full of egoism and self-love, souls full of pride and arrogance, souls full of deceit and hypocrisy, lukewarm souls who have just enough warmth to keep them alive: My Heart can not bear this. All of the graces that I pour out upon them flow off them as off the face of a rock. I cannot stand them, because they are neither good nor bad. I called convents into being to sanctify the world through them. It is from them that a powerful flame of love and sacrifice should burst forth. Moreover, if they do not repent and become enkindled by their first love, I will deliver them over to the fate of this world... How can they sit on the promised throne of judgment to judge the world, when their guilt is greater than the guilt of the world? There is neither penance nor atonement. O heart, which received Me in the morning and at noon are all ablaze with hatred against Me, hatred of all sorts! O heart specially chosen by Me, were you chosen for this, to give Me more pain? The great sins of the world are superficial wounds on My heart, but the sins of a chosen soul pierce My Heart through and through...

—Diary entry 1702

Faustina—possibly as a result of her own treatment inside the convent walls—tried but failed to excuse this sort of behavior. As she described in her diary, she was unable to think of anything in the defense of those against whom Christ was bringing a charge.

As a result she describes her heart being seized with pain, and she wept bitterly. Then as she recorded the incident, Jesus in His compassion comforted her;

> *Do not cry. There are still a number of souls, who love Me very much, but My heart desires to be loved by all and, because My love is great, that is why I warn and chastise them.*

> **—Diary entry 1703**

Christ also explained to Faustina how someone consumed by sin or guilt should approach Him and receive mercy.

Be not afraid of YOUR Savior, O sinful soul. I make the first move to come to you, for I know that by yourself, you are unable to lift yourself to Me. Child, do not run away from Your Father; be willing to talk openly with your God of mercy who wants to speak words of pardon and lavish his graces on you. How dear your soul is to Me! I have inscribed your name upon My hand; you are engraved as a deep wound in My Heart.

As her spiritual Director continued to listen to these messages, it became evident that there was a larger plan at stake here. Father Sopocko soon realized that these messages were not just intended for Faustina but for the whole world. Upon ascertaining the universal importance of what was being told to her Sopocko instructed Faustina to keep a record of the encounters and her unique spiritual journey, which she would obediently write down in a diary. It is quite fascinating that two diaries would emerge from Europe during the first half of the Twentieth Century. One from a young girl called Anne Frank who wrote about the Nazi Occupation and the horrors of the past. The other journal penned by Faustina who wrote about the future and God's plan for mankind.

CHAPTER SEVEN

THE DIARY

My daughter, I demand that you devote all your free time to writing about My goodness and mercy.

—Diary entry 1567

My daughter, be diligent in writing down every sentence I tell you concerning My mercy, because this is meant for a great number of souls who will profit from it.

—Diary entry 1142

Four years prior to her death, Faustina's spiritual director Father Sopocko told her to keep a record of her encounters with Christ in a Diary. It was a suggestion that would be fully endorsed by Christ Himself who also instructed Faustina to write down everything He told her. **"Write these words on a clean sheet of paper: From today on, my own will does not exist,"** **and then cross out the page. And on the other side write these words: "From today on, I will do the will of God everywhere, always, and in everything."** - Diary entry 374

The importance of *The Diary* can best be measured if we consider a world without it. There would be no record of Christ's communications with Faustina—no detailed account of His message for mankind—and the Pontificate of Pope John Paul II would have taken an entirely different direction. It is therefore in this context that we are able to see why this Diary is so significant and also why *The Image* instructed to Faustina is one, which the world needs to see.

Faustina started writing the Diary on July 28, 1934. It begins with beautifully lyrical words and continues with messages that would continue over a seven year period. **"I am to write down the encounters of my soul with You, O God, at the moments of Your special visitations." (Diary entry 6)** It is evident from her writing that Faustina was aware that this would be no easy task. Yet she remained faithful to the end as God's grace sustained her.

> *O incomprehensible in mercy towards my poor soul. Your Holy will is the life of my soul. I have received this order through him who is Your representative here on earth, who interprets Your Holy will to me. Jesus, You see how difficult it is for me to write, how unable I am to put down clearly what I experience in my soul. O God, can a pen write down that for which many a time there are no words? But You give the order to write, O God, that is enough for me.*

—Diary entry 6

Faustina's writings have been proven to assure us that they come from God, for there could be no other explanation as to how this poor uneducated, yet devoutly pious woman could have written a dialog of over six hundred pages, with a fountain pen, and deliver a manuscript which had no corrections and flowed like silk. Certainly the time spent in writing this Diary caused much annoyance amongst her fellow sisters who could not understand why this uneducated member of their community was allowed so much time to put down her thoughts. What could Faustina possibly be penning that anyone would want to read? Her time could have been allotted for housework or other chores they felt would have contributed more to the community.

We now know that *The Diary* is in fact the only resource the Church would later have to understand Faustina's mission. The assignment to make the world aware of *The Divine Mercy of God*, have *The Image* of the Merciful Jesus painted, and install *The Feast of Divine Mercy* on the Sunday following Easter.

> *No soul will be justified until it turns with confidence*
> *to My mercy; and this is why the first Sunday after Easter*
> *is to be the Feast of Mercy, and on that day, priests are to*
> *tell everyone about My great and unfathomable mercy.*
>
> **—Diary entry 570**

The *Diary* would also outline Christ's instructions to introduce a special prayer to the Church and indeed to the whole world. *The Chaplet of The Divine Mercy* was to be said at three o'clock every day. It is a prayer that appeals to the shed blood of Jesus for atonement. It is a prayer that Pope John Paul II ultimately would never fail to pray and one which he implored the Universal Church to likewise follow suit. According to Christ's instruction, those who recite this Chaplet are to offer to God the Father "the body and blood, Soul and Divinity," of Jesus Christ in atonement for their sins, the sins of their loved ones, and those of the entire world. This action was to be carried out at the hour of Christ's death:

> *as often as you hear the clock strike the third hour,*
> *immense yourself completely in My mercy, adoring and*
> *glorifying it; invoke its omnipotence for the whole world,*
> *and particularly poor sinners; for at that moment mercy*
> *was opened wide for every soul.*
>
> **—Diary entry 1572**

So great was God's desire that His words to Faustina be preserved, that there is a constant theme throughout *The Diary* of Christ requesting that these uniquely spiritual encounters which He shared with Faustina be preserved. This of course suggests that a printed record of this dialog would one day be needed for a larger purpose. One possible explanation as to why Christ was emphatic that she not miss a word is understood in the following words:

> *You have not written anything in the notebook about*
> *My goodness towards humankind; I desire that you omit*
> *nothing; I desire that your heart be firmly grounded in*
> *total peace.*
>
> **—Diary entry 459**

Throughout these Divine dialogues it was quite apparent that these words were not intended exclusively for Faustina but for humanity as a whole and she was the messenger:

> *My daughter, you do not live for yourself but for souls; write for their benefit. You know that My will as to your writing has been confirmed many times by your confessors. You know what is pleasing to Me, and if you have any doubts about what I am saying, you also know whom you are to ask.*
>
> — **Diary entry 895**

Christ also warned Faustina of the consequences of not being obedient to His promptings.

> *Souls perish in spite of My bitter Passion. I am giving them the last hope of salvation; that is, the Feast of My Mercy. If they will not adore My Mercy, they will perish for all eternity. Secretary of My mercy, write; tell souls about this great mercy of Mine, because the awful day, the day of My justice, is near.*
>
> —**Diary entry 965**

It is evident from the way the instructions were given, that the enormity of the task given to Faustina was a completely global and universal directive. God's plan was clear. It would be penned by Faustina, endorsed by Pope John Paul II, and eventually made available on an international scale after the turn of this century when Faustina had been made a Saint.

> *Apostle of My mercy, proclaim to the whole world My unfathomable mercy. Do not be discouraged by the difficulties you encounter in proclaiming My mercy. These difficulties that affect you so painfully are needed for your sanctification and as evidence that this work is mine. My daughter, be diligent in writing down every sentence I tell you concerning My mercy, because this is meant for a great number of souls who will profit from it.*
>
> —**Diary entry 1142**

Everything Faustina undertook regarding the writing of *The Diary* required the same spiritual attitude as she applied to prayer. Each time she approached the task of writing, she would ask God to **"Bless this Pen,"** This was not surprising given her limited education. Writing did not come easy to Faustina, which may have been the reason she was chosen for this assignment. If Faustina had great literary ability, the content and the motive behind the exercise, which lasted seven years, could have been called into question. Instead it was the mystical and sustained dimension of this dialog that was written by such an uneducated nun that prompted the expert theologians to assess the documents as evidencing God's guiding hand in all of it.

While *The Diary* chronicles her life, it is not a historical journal, but a spiritual one. Though she talks about members of her community, the main emphasis of the journal is clearly on her conversations with Christ; a detailed and verbatim account of everything that He told her. The purpose of *The Diary* was also not to show what a sublime connection she had to God or how particularly holy she was, but rather was a straight forward reiteration of what was happening in her soul and the struggles she encountered along with the graces she received and the messages she was intended to share with the world.

Divided into five notebooks today, the Church considers *The Diary*, one of the greatest pieces of mystical literature. *The Diary* provides a journey of a completely supernatural nature which Pope John Paul read frequently. It clearly was not written to make Faustina the heroine but rather reveals her own weaknesses, failings, and general incompetence in spiritual matters. Every line is penned with honesty and love. The overriding theme of the book is a warning and invitation to trust in God and to be prepared for His final coming.

While some experts on mystical literature believe the book contains a generic theme, clearly Pope John Paul II's insistence that these messages were of vital importance to the whole world suggests a real need related to the historical context of where humanity sits today. A place, it seems that, is capable of the most marvelous achievements and the very worst potential for genuine self-destruction.

Through *The Diary* the depth of Faustina's spiritual life is revealed and in reading it, one is able to begin to understand just how close she was to God as well as her absolute faith in Him. It is because of that faith that the Church would ultimately believe the messages contained in *The Diary*. Additionally, the Diary also reveals her visions, revelations, hidden stigmata, gift of prophecy, and her ability to read human souls. In fact, within *The Diary*, Faustina herself acknowledges that it is not these many unique gifts that made her holy, but simply her faith in God. This was something that also convinced the Church:

> *Neither graces, nor revelations, nor raptures, nor gifts granted to a soul make it perfect, but rather the intimate union of the soul with God… My sanctity and perfection is based upon the close union of my will with the will of God.*

Diary entry 1107

Far from being a work of self-indulgence, as her fellow sisters suspected, Faustina was clearly on a mission assigned by God to remind us of His love for man. Through *The Diary*, Jesus wanted to proclaim His message of mercy to the whole world: *"Today,"* He told her:

> *I am sending you with My mercy to the people of the whole world. I do not want to punish aching mankind, but I desire to heal it, pressing it to My merciful Heart." "You are the secretary of My mercy; I have chosen you for that office in this life and the next life.*

Diary entry 1605

Since Faustina's death in 1938 and following her Canonization in 2000, it certainly seems that the office chosen for her by God goes on. In May of 2006, on one of his first foreign visits as Pope, Benedict XV1, visited Faustina's tomb and prayed. Sadly, many within the Church do not realize *The Diary's* spiritual significance or recognize The Image as a Vessel of grace. Which begs the question as to why the endorsement of Pope John Paul II should not warrant the need for this all to be thoroughly considered?

Chapter Eight

Diary Destroyed

My daughter; write that the greater the misery of a soul, the greater its right to My mercy; [urge] all souls to trust in the unfathomable abyss of My mercy, because I want to save them all.

—Diary entry 1182

It is impossible to fully understand all that was going on at times in Sister Faustina's mind. It seems that despite the extraordinary graces that were being bestowed upon her, she nevertheless occasionally experienced a great torment in her soul. For while she was evidently communicating in a unique way with God and helping to carry out what she believed was His Divine Plan for mankind, she also experienced little encouragement from those around her. As a result she was becoming something of a dichotomy even to herself. Here was unquestionably an immensely interior and solitary soul, but one whose beautiful exterior personality attracted many to her. Faustina was also a humble servant and an obedient nun, yet also one who felt compelled to start her own religious order and even seriously considered going to Rome to visit the Pope in order to discuss the mission entrusted to her by God.

Certainly many around Faustina were at times quite confused as to where she was coming from. They began to question whether her motives were mystical or manipulative—or perhaps even malevolent. Because we now understand that she was most certainly inspired by God, it is easy to forgive those around her for their inability to realize this.

As has been previously discussed, the one man who did take her seriously was her spiritual director, Father Michael Sopocko. This holy priest first met Faustina in 1933, and would remain her confessor until her death. As Fr Sopocko remembered:

> *I met Sister Faustina in the summer of 1933 (in July or August) – she was a penitent in the Congregation of Sisters of Our Lady of Mercy in Vilnius where I was a regular confessor at the time. She drew my attention by her extraordinary subtlety and close communion with God: in the majority of cases, there were no grounds for absolution as she never offended God with a mortal sin. Right from the very beginning, she declared that she knows me from some vision she had and that I am to be the spiritual director of her conscience and must help her realize some of God's plans which are to be specified by her. I ignored this tale of hers and decided to put her to a test; as a result, with permission of Mother Superior, sister Faustina began to look for another confessor. After some time she came back to me and declared that she is prepared to bear everything but that she will never leave me.*

As we have learned, Father Sopocko would play a vital role in the mission entrusted to Faustina. It would be this pious priest who told her to keep a Diary and who had *The Image* commissioned. He would also be the one who started to petition the Church authorities to install *The Feast of Divine Mercy* and he also penned a series of articles which outlined the importance of this devotion.

This was a tremendous undertaking for a man who already had an extremely busy life dedicated to God. Without the mission of assisting

Faustina, Father Sopocko was already a parish priest, a catechist, an educator, a teacher, a University and Seminary lecturer, a spiritual father, confessor to seminary students, priests and nuns, an army chaplain, a sobriety activist as well as a founder and builder of churches. Certainly Father Sopocko's selection by God to be the man who would help carry out Faustina's mission may have been because he had devoted his entire life in the service of God. The bond which existed between Faustina and this priest provided her with great comfort and encouragement in executing her mission. From Faustina's viewpoint, here was a man of God who did take her seriously and was even prepared to help her.

Between 1936, to her death in 1938, Faustina would write a number of letters to her spiritual father; the majority of which were sent from the convent in Krakow. In total she wrote 19 letters to Father Sopocko and he wrote 7 letters in response to hers. It is evident from the correspondence that Faustina, despite her limited schooling had mastered the art of letter-writing. It is also apparent the letters were an extension of her spiritual encounters and she began each one with the sign of the cross and an abbreviation "J.M.J." (Jesus, Mary, Joseph) placed in the left upper corner. In the upper right hand corner or at the foot of the page, Faustina would put the name of the place that she was writing from and the date. She addressed all of her letters with great reverence using various titles. "Reverend Father", "Dearest Father", "Most Reverend Father."

Each letter usually begins with details of her current situation and the problems that she was experiencing in her daily life. She frequently discussed her health and the state of her soul, but the overriding theme was concern about the mission Christ had imparted to her. Each letter always ended politely "I kiss your hand Father and entreat you for prayers and God's blessing" or, "With deepest respect I kiss your hands, Dear Father and send you my greetings in the Lord – Sister Faustina."

The style of the letters is in many ways similar to *The Diary*. She writes with great sincerity and according to Rev. Jan Machniak who has carefully studied the letters, "In her letters, Saint Faustina gave systematic accounts of the development of her spiritual life. She wrote about her great longing to become united with God."

Clearly when she did not have access to Father Sopocko physically, these letters provided a much necessary spiritual outlet. A means whereby sister Faustina could still express what was happening in her soul to her spiritual director. Yet the long absences from the man she considered Christ's representative on earth did have an adverse effect on her. At one point, such was her despair that the mission she was undertaking appeared to fall apart.

Father Sopocko's dedication to Faustina's mission cannot be questioned but this was not his only role in life. An extremely busy man, he was often called upon to travel long distances both in Poland and overseas as well. At every juncture however, he stressed to Faustina the importance of maintaining *The Diary* and also ensuring its safekeeping. It is difficult to know what prompted Faustina to start doubting her mission to such an extent that she no longer wanted to maintain *The Diary*, but evaluators believe it may have been the work of the devil. In 1934, with Father Sopocko on a trip to the Holy Land and Faustina's ability to communicate with him curtailed, she began to hate *The Diary* and the hold that it had on her. One day, believing it was God's will, she burnt *The Diary*—along with all of the records of the experiences of her soul. Likewise, Christ's messages for the world appeared lost forever.

Devastated upon learning the news, Father Sopocko instructed her to rewrite the journal. It seemed an impossible task but ultimately one that would prove God's hand was involved. Faustina picked up her pen and began the document again. Mysteriously, as the investigation into the canonization process would ultimately reveal the contents did not contradict the original. In fact every episode was recounted in the very same way. If ever there was a question mark as to her stories authenticity here was final confirmation that the communications from Christ were identical to the ones that she had initially described.

Chapter Nine

A Holy Death

Your death will be a solemn one and I will accompany you in that last hour.

—Diary entry 1061

Throughout her religious life, Faustina had been plagued by physical and spiritual sufferings. At times it seemed as though she was sustained only by her faith and a resolve to complete her task here on earth. By August of 1938 however, her health had deteriorated to such a degree that it seemed unlikely she would live long enough to see her mission accomplished. Yet many people were starting to see the value of this humble sister and her very special role in a Divine plan In fact, in an ironic twist having been subjected to many years of ridicule and humiliation, in her time of great suffering the sisters at her convent began to recognize her holiness and appealed for her to intercede for them in prayer.

When Mother Michael, Faustina's Superior, heard the sad news of Faustina's illness, she wrote to her obedient nun, assuring Faustina of her sympathy and remembrance. Faustina in turn penned her own reply in which she admitted that the tuberculosis had indeed begun to take its final toll:

Dearest Mother, it seems to me that this is our last conversation on earth. I am very weak, and am writing with trembling hand. I am suffering as much as I can stand. Jesus does not give beyond our strength. I rely completely on God and His holy will. An even greater yearning for God encompasses me. Death does not frighten me; my soul abounds in deep peace. I shall make all my spiritual exercises. I shall also rise for Mass, but do not remain to the end because I feel ill. However, I take advantage of the graces Jesus left us in His Church as best I can. Dearest Mother, I thank you, from a heart overwhelmed with deep gratitude, for all the good I received in the community, from the first moment I entered until now. I especially thank you, Mother, for your heartfelt compassion and direction in difficult times, seemingly impossible to endure. May God repay you abundantly! Now, in the spirit of religious humility, I most humbly beg pardon of you, Dearest Mother, for my inexact keeping of the rules, for any bad example I may have given to the sisters, for lack of zeal in my entire religious life, for all the troubles and sufferings I may have unknowingly caused you, Mother. Your goodness was my strength, loving Mother, in trying times…. Good-bye, Dearest Mother, we shall see each other in heaven at the foot of God's throne. And now, may The Divine Mercy be glorified in us and through us… The greatest misery and nothingness, Sister Faustina.

Very shortly after this letter was written, Sister Faustina wrote about a glimpse she had of what would become of *The Divine Mercy* devotion after her death:

> *Today I saw the glory of God which flows from the image. Many souls are receiving graces, although they do not speak of it openly. Even though it has met with all sorts of vicissitudes, God is receiving glory because of it; and the efforts of Satan and of evil men are shattered and come to naught. In spite of Satan's anger, The Divine Mercy will triumph over the whole world and will be worshipped by all souls.*
>
> **—Diary entry 1789**

On August 24th, Sister Faustina took a turn for the worst and death seemed imminent. The next day, her thirty third birthday, she was given the last Rites, and a few days later, still barely clinging to life, she was visited by Father Sopocko who witnessed the absolute peace which surrounded her. Faustina appeared to Sopocko as if she was in ecstasy, no longer communing with earth but with heaven. At this point Faustina, who was staying at the infirmary, was asked by the sister assigned to care for her if she would like to return to the community to die. With a joyful smile Faustina said, "I won't die yet, so please let me stay here. I will be a burden to the community." However, she also added, "But please, do what you think is best, and what the superiors wish."

Two weeks later, Faustina was taken home to the convent. Realizing how frail she was, Sister Afreda who was helping transport her became alarmed. Faustina tried to alleviate her fears, "Sister, please don't worry, because I will not die on the way."

Once back in her own cell at the convent in Lagiewniki, Faustina received tender loving care from Sister Amelia. By this time, she had become so weak that she could no longer eat food and with her health slowly fading away, according to Convent custom on September 22, Faustina asked pardon of the entire community. Four days later, Father Sopocko would make his last visit to her. He found that Sister no longer had any cause to confess to him. "She gives the impression of an unearthly being. I no longer have the least doubt that what is found in her diary, concerning Holy Communion being administered by an angel, is true." It was at this juncture that Faustina would reveal the exact date of her death. This would mark her last prophetic revelation to Father Sopocko. Yet right up until she drew her last breath, Faustina would continue to impart prophecies to her fellow sisters. In fact, a few days before she died, one sister, Sr. Gardener who visited her and inquired "Aren't you afraid of death, sister?" "Why?" came Faustina's reply. "All my sins and imperfections will be consumed like straw in the fire of Divine Mercy." They then discussed the pending war and Sister Gardener apparently suggested that it would be a short battle. In another moment of prophecy, Faustina explained that the outcome would be quite different. " The war will be terribly long, long, long. There will be much misfortune; terrible sufferings will come upon the people."

"Will Poland still exist?" inquired the sister.

"Oh Poland will exist, but there will be few people left because many will perish. And they will love each other much and will desire to see each other."

Frequently Faustina would ask her fellow sisters to pray for Poland. Many of them could not understand her concern about the pending war. Ironically, following her death, the war would begin and the sisters would be threatened by eviction from the Nazis. Each time the threat loomed, they would pray *The Chaplet of Divine Mercy* and ask for Faustina's intercession. On every occasion their prayers were answered.

In the last moments of her life, many of the sisters gathered around Faustina. Finally her true heroic value and holiness was being recognized. Despite her terrible physical condition, Faustina spoke of *The Feast of Divine Mercy* and its coming to fruition. She even predicted to the sisters that, "You will see; the congregation will have much joy because of me." It seemed she wanted to offer a gift of hope even during her own suffering. She was right; today the convent attracts visitors from all over the world and in the past decade has been graced with Papal visits from Pope John Paul II as well as Benedict XVI. Among her last predictions was the one she confided to Mother Irene. "The Lord Jesus wants to elevate me and make me a Saint." It would happen 62 years later.

It was a moment of great sadness when on October 5, 1938; Faustina whispered to Sister Felicia, "The Lord will take me today." Because she was suffering so severely, an injection to ease the pain was ordered, but Faustina refused, wanting instead to fulfill God's will to the end. At Nine O'clock, her sisters gathered around her bed and started praying. Joined by a priest, Father Czaputa at 10.45, Faustina her eyes raised to heaven went to her reward.

At her funeral two days later on October 7, 1938, there were five priests, three of whom were Jesuits and a cleric who each presided at the Mass in the convent chapel attended by her entire congregation. Today it is at that same location where thousands gather to see *The Image* that now hangs to the left of the altar and to pray over the relics of this holy woman. Sadly, it was Faustina's dying wish that her family would not be told of her death or the funeral until after she was buried. Faustina was concerned that they not incur the expense of traveling to say goodbye. It was a sad yet fitting end for this woman who had spent a lifetime putting the feelings and needs of others before her own. In fact, Sister Faustina did countless works of mercy throughout her short time on earth right up until her moment of death. She did this even though she was plagued by suffering from tuberculosis—a fact that she kept hidden for years from her community. Even her Mother Superior did not realize how sick she was, and as she suffered in silence, such was her humanity that Faustina constantly prayed for those who were dying, though she also was in great pain and dying herself.

Part Two:

Maria Faustina Kowalska and Karol Wojtyla - A Friendship Made In Heaven

CHAPTER TEN

DIVINE PROVIDENCE

Even as a young man, Pope John Paul II had a strong connection to the legend of Saint Faustina. Born Karol Józef Wojtyła, eighteen years prior to her death, having heard about the life of this great mystic, he would frequently pass by her convent and pray at her tomb. There was, it seems, something about this woman's life that drew young Karol Wojtyla to her and prompted him to seek her intercession through prayer. Because of the times that young Karol lived through, there was much for this young man to pray for. Born May 18, 1920, Karol was the youngest of three children born to Karol Wojtyła and Emilia Kaczorowska. In 1929, at the tender age of nine, Karol was devastated by the death of his mother. This was one of a number of family tragedies. Before Karol was born, his sister Olga had died while still very young and this would not be the only death of one of the children born into this family. The late Pontiff's eldest brother Edmund, a doctor, also died only three years after the death of their mother in 1932. To add to this young man's pain, Karol's father, a non-commissioned army officer died in 1941. Sadly, for the man who would ultimately bring so much joy to the world, at the age of twenty-one, the future Pope had lost everyone he loved. At this moment he entrusted his life to the Virgin Mary and found comfort in faith.

Baptized on June 20, 1920 in the parish church of Wadowice by Fr. Franciszek Zak, he made his First Holy Communion at age 9 and was confirmed at 18. Upon graduation from Marcin Wadowita high school in Wadowice, Karol enrolled in Krakow's Jagiellonian University in 1938 and in a school for drama.

The Nazi occupation forces closed the university in 1939 and the young Karol had to work in a quarry (1940-1944) and then in the Solvay chemical factory to earn his living and to avoid being deported to Germany. It was at this juncture, having no close family to turn to and with the world around him in turmoil, young Karol found comfort at Faustina's convent and prayed to her. There is a measure of irony in the fact that years later, he would become Pope and officiate her canonization. Yet, despite everything that was happening around him, in his youth and then later in his role as Pope, he still continued to pray to Faustina. Indeed, by 1942, Karol's prayers seemed answered, when he became aware of his call to the priesthood. Shortly afterwards, he began courses in the clandestine seminary of Krakow, run by Cardinal Adam Stefan Sapieha, archbishop of Krakow. At the same time, Karol Wojtyła was one of the pioneers of the "Rhapsodic Theatre," also clandestine.

Young Wojtyla certainly kept himself busy. He worked as a volunteer librarian and did compulsory military training in the Academic Legion. In his youth the man who would be Pope was extremely well rounded becoming an athlete, actor, and playwright. This was a man who would go on to know as many as twelve languages, including Latin, Ukrainian, Greek, Spanish, Portuguese, French, Italian, German, English, and of course his native Polish. Wojtyla also had some facility with Russian.

After the Second World War, Karol continued his studies in the major seminary of Krakow, once it had re-opened, and in the faculty of theology of the Jagiellonian University. He was ordained to the priesthood by Archbishop Sapieha in Krakow on November 1, 1946.

Meanwhile, Faustina's mission to make the message and the Image known throughout the world was not going well and Christ's instructions to Faustina had not been fulfilled. By the early 1950's, all mention of devotion to her prayer and the Image had virtually disappeared from Catholic Churches in Poland. In addition, with the war over, the Polish people had to begin to rebuild their country and bringing attention to the contents of Faustina's Diary seemed to be a last priority.

Shortly following Karol's ordination, Cardinal Sapieha sent him to Rome where he worked under the guidance of the French Dominican, Garrigou-Lagrange. He finished his doctorate in theology in 1948 with a thesis on the subject of faith in the works of St. John of the Cross (*Doctrina de fide apud Sanctum Ioannem a Cruce*). During his vacations, Karol exercised his pastoral ministry among the Polish immigrants of France, Belgium, and Holland. In 1948, he returned to Poland and was vicar of various parishes in Krakow as well as chaplain to university students. This period lasted until 1951 when he again took up his studies in philosophy and theology. In 1953, he defended a thesis on "evaluation of the possibility of founding a Catholic ethic on the ethical system of German Philospher Max Scheler" at Lublin Catholic University. Later he became professor of moral theology and social ethics in the major seminary of Krakow and in the Faculty of Theology of Lublin. On July 4, 1958, Karol was appointed titular bishop of Ombi and auxiliary of Krakow by Pope Pius XII, and was consecrated September 28, 1958, in Wawel Cathedral, Krakow, by Archbishop Eugeniusz Baziak. On January 13, 1964, he was appointed archbishop of Krakow by Pope Paul VI, who made him a cardinal on June 26, 1967 with the title of S. Cesareo in Palatio of the order of deacons, later elevated pro illa vice to the order of priests.

In what can only be seen as Divine providence, when John Paul became Cardinal, Faustina's position as the forgotten mystic looked set for change. Convinced Faustina had a message for humanity, the Cardinal, who would soon be Pope earnestly began starting the process to make her a Saint. It is conceivable that his devotion to Faustina was prompted by his own prayers to her being miraculously and continuously answered. Whatever the reason, we do know that throughout his priesthood, he remained adamant about making Faustina a Saint, even though at times it seemed an impossible task.

To begin the Canonization process, he approached an expert theologian and asked him to assess all of her writings. In turn the theologian was presented with *The Diary* along with various letters. Yet the theologian clearly did not share the Cardinal's enthusiasm or understand the importance of such a mission. Instead this scripture scholar placed the file on his desk and left it sitting there for years. This act of indifference would later go to form the content of this scholars introduction to his eventual thesis on Faustina's writings. Indeed, after subsequent reading of her work, he asked for forgiveness for his actions and indifference. In fact he begins his study with great humility and honesty:

> *The author of the following theological study confesses that during more than one quarter of the century he was very suspicious about the heroical sainthood of Helen Faustina, and mostly about the revelations that she had been favored to receive. He believed himself authorized to think this way because he had heard from initiators in the cause of Helen Faustina among which were Monsignor Stanislas Rospond auxiliary Bishop of Krakow and one of the priest confessors of Faustina. In the opinion of the author, Helen Faustina, a very pious and simple girl was victim of hallucinations of hysterical origin and as such the so called revelations were lacking in religious value. Because of such assessment he doubted the heroic value of her life. This prejudice was the source of the categorical refusal by the author to participate as an expert theologian in the process of beatification started by Cardinal Karol Wojtyla Archbishop of Krakow for Sister Faustina. His negative attitude began to change when out of simple human curiosity, to kill time; he began to skip through the Petit Journal (Diary). His opinion was shaken by the future examination of the document. A careful and methodical rereading followed resulting in the conclusion that the case of Helen Faustina deserved a more rigorous and scientific study. This last one, third in chronological order, convinced the author of the following:*

> *First, the data on which the former initiators, had in the past, modeled their negative attitude was incomplete, incorrect or false.*

> *Second. The Sainthood of Helen Faustina, is truly heroic and her revelations carry all signs of supernatural origin. Third. Having arrived to the highest degree of scientific certainty the author has the inescapable duty to give written testimony. The author offers the fruit of his labor to the*

infinite, eternal, and incarnate mercy of God, to thank Him
for all his blessings and to ask for forgiveness of his sins.

In what could be best described as a literary and theological autopsy, the author painstakingly reviewed literally every aspect of Faustina's writings. His mission was to form an idea about the message to the world that she had been given her basis for Sainthood and her mystical abilities. Every word, sentence structure and handwriting were examined to determine whether she was indeed a woman of God. By the author's own admission, if the revelation didn't come from God but were the product of a morbid imagination or the result of illusion created by a malevolent spirit Helen Faustina would have been an unlikely person, victim of her own imagination or that of a malevolent spirit. Could we then award tribute to her authentic Sainthood and heroism in conforming to the will of Christ and in accordance with a perfect spiritual assimilation with God? The answer seems clear.

Line by line *The Diary* was studied, all with a series of questions in mind. Where these messages from God? Was Faustina's life one of true and heroic sanctity? Does she exhibit through the writings, true mystical phenomenon? In addition, do her writings correspond to the moral and dogmatic teachings of the Church? Furthermore, are the contents of the diary simply a memoir where she is recounting her daily life or does it contain messages for the Church Universal and indeed for all mankind?

The theologian further points out that *The Diary* having not been written for publication and intended to be a secret until after Faustina's death, was certainly not written with any motive in mind. He further points out that evident throughout her writings is Faustina's great "moral honesty." How her written prayers delight us by their honesty but they also point out that every man is imperfect. "If the author of a diary writes his own true story only, he will also write about his imperfections, facts that show him at a disadvantage. If he does not, he would be neither sincere nor honest. In the Diary there are in effect a number of revelations disadvantageous for Faustina and it is for us a sign that she writes only truth."

What is also interesting to note is how one Diary and a collection of letters was used to form the basis of Faustina's sainthood. Visits from Christ and the Mother of God were clearly something this expert

79

theologian assessed sceptically. Faustina's writing style also added to the problem and the task of assessing the supernatural value of her documents was made from a highly suspicious standpoint. After all, the contents of her Diary were a consoling, yet frightening direct message from Christ to prepare the world for His return. As a result, the assessment was a sort of positive negative. On one hand, everything she stated was true yet on the other hand it forced the questions as to how, when and where was all this pointing?

There was only one man who really seemed to know the answer and in what must be viewed as Divine providence, he would take the findings of the study to his new job at the Vatican.

Chapter Eleven

The Cardinal becomes Pope

At approximately 5:15 p.m. on October 16, 1978, Cardinal Karol Wojtyla was elected the 264th Sucsessor of Peter. His appointment, following the death of Pope John I who had reigned for only thirty-three days, was viewed by many as something of a groundbreaking move. He was after all, a Polish pontiff and not an Italian; the first non- Italian Pope in over 400 years.

Only 58 years of age, he was also the youngest pope elected since Pope Pius IX in 1846. Like his immediate predecessor, John Paul I, John Paul II dispensed with the traditional Papal coronation and instead received ecclesiastical investiture with the simplified Papal inauguration on October 22, 1978. During the ceremony when one of the cardinals knelt before him, took their vows, and went to kiss his ring as was the custom the Pope stood up as the Polish primate Stefan Cardinal Wyszynski knelt down and stopped him from kissing the ring, and hugged him instead. It was a move indicative of the approachable style in which he would govern. He would be accessible and human.

This charismatic Pole's style was not only unconventional but as the youngest Pope of the 20th Century he would become the most media friendly Pope of all time and one well aware that he was confronted with a changing world.

John Paul II would also learn to grow in the role for while his career—although rapid—had not been a spectacular one, and while respected, he was little known outside of Vatican circles. Yet ultimately, his style won him hearts around the world.

Indeed, few experts had even considered Karol as a successor to Pope John Paul I. Yet as things would transpire this would be the right man at the right time and his would be one of the most glorious Papacies in the history of the Catholic Church. As we know, Pope John Paul II would become the most traveled and most well known figure ever to spring from the Vatican and a man who would handle global issues like no other Pontiff in history.

In fact, right from the start, Pope John Paul II was clearly determined to show God's love to the whole world. Yet there was one assignment which for him stood above all else and which he considered his special mission. For while it would take twenty-two years to achieve it, he publicly stated this was his major task:

> *Right from the beginning of my ministry in St. Peter's See in Rome, I considered this message my special task. Providence has assigned it to me in the present situation of man, the Church, and the world.*

It is hard to imagine what would have happened to Faustina's canonization if another Pope unfamiliar with her story had taken office. We do know however that prior to Pope John Paul's arrival, canonizing this Polish mystic was not on the Holy See's agenda. Now however, there was a new man in charge and one who seemed to have a greater understanding of Sister Faustina Kowalska's mission than did any other pontifical candidate. Was this all part of the Divine plan—that a Polish Pope would be elected to deliver the messages of a Polish mystic to mankind? Certainly in the history of the Church, no one else has been so insistent on the importance of her messages.

It was also true that no Pope in Vatican history had received the same level of international attention and media exposure as John Paul II. Apart from his academic genius, this was a man who reached out to everyone and Vatican relations with people of all faiths flourished under his Papacy. Pope John Paul II was not just the head of the Roman Catholic Church but a spiritual father figure to the world. Here was a man who would reach out to the world, and who would ultimately entrust the world to the message of Divine Mercy.

In order to fulfill his mission and deliver this global message the Pontiff was particularly keen to bridge the gap between people of all faiths. Pope John Paul II was also well aware of the divisions previously created by the Catholic Church, the reality of the Crusades, the painful memory of the Spanish inquisition, and the suffering of the Jews during World War II. To achieve his goal of inter-faith dialog John Paul traveled extensively throughout his Papacy, and became one of the most widely traveled Popes in history. During his reign he came into contact with believers from many divergent faiths and his mission was clear as he constantly attempted to find common ground, both doctrinal and dogmatic in order to bring unity within the entire human family. Pope John Paul genuinely reached out to all people irrespective of their belief system, nationality, color, creed, or gender.... One example of this was World Day of Prayer for Peace, held in Assisi on October 27, 1986, where more than 120 representatives of different religions and Christian denominations spent a day together fasting and praying.

John Paul was particularly keen to improve relations between Catholics and Jews. As Pope he spoke frequently about the Church's relationship with Jews, a subject dear to his heart as he was deeply pained at the suffering of the Jewish people during World War II.

As a child, Karol Wojtyla had played sports with his many Jewish neighbors, they were his friends, and he was tormented by the holocaust much of which was carried out in his native homeland. Such was his sorrow as to what happened in Poland that in 1979 he became the first Pope to visit Auschwitz concentration camp a place not far from his childhood home and where many of his countrymen (mostly Polish Jews) perished during the German Nazi occupation.

Not only was John Paul II the first pope to have made an official visit to a synagogue, when he visited the Synagogue of Rome on 13 April 1986 but he also expressed the Church's remorse over its failure to embrace Judaism over the years.

Additionally, in March 2000, John Paul II visited Yad Vashem, (the Israeli national Holocaust memorial) in Israel and later made history by touching Judaism's holiest site the Western Wall in Jerusalem. While on that visit the Pope placed a letter inside it (in which he apologized for the Church's actions against Jews in the past). One of the leading Israeli newspapers said simply, in gratified amazement, 'A man of God has walked among us'.

So well received were the Pontiff's actions that in October 2003 the Anti-Defamation League (ADL) issued a statement congratulating John Paul II on entering the 25th year of his distinguished Pontificate. In addition immediately after the pope's death in 2005, the ADL said that he had revolutionized Catholic-Jewish relations, saying that "more change for the better took place in his 27 year Papacy than in the nearly 2,000 years before." (*Pope John Paul II: An Appreciation: A Visionary Remembered*).

The late pontiff also extended his spiritual diplomacy to the Eastern Orthodox Church when in May 1999, John Paul II visited Romania on the invitation from Patriarch Teoctist of the Romanian Orthodox Church. This was the first time a pope had visited a predominantly Eastern Orthodox country since the Great Schism in 1054.

On his arrival, the Patriarch and the President of Romania, Emil Constantinescu, greeted the Pope. The Patriarch stated, "The second millennium of Christian history began with a painful wounding of the unity of the Church; the end of this millennium has seen a real commitment to restoring Christian unity."

John Paul II visited other heavily Orthodox areas such as Ukraine, despite a lack of welcome at times, and he said that an end to the Schism was one of his fondest wishes. The Pope said throughout his pontificate that one of his greatest dreams was to visit Russia, but sadly this never occurred. He had even made several attempts to solve the problems which arose over a period of centuries between the Roman Catholic and Russian Orthodox churches, like giving back the icon of Our Lady of Kazan, in August 2004. However, the Orthodox Church never expressed much enthusiasm, making statements to the effect of: "The question of the visit of the Pope in Russia is not connected by the journalists with the problems between the Churches, which are now unreal to solve, but with giving back one of many sacred things, which were illegally stolen from Russia."

The late Pontiff's efforts to create and unify the human family were not just confined to Europe. He also extended himself globally especially with Tenzin Gyatso, the 14th Dalai Lama and the spiritual leader of Tibetan Buddhism. The Dalai Lama's eight visits to the Vatican outnumbered the visits of any other single dignitary. These two men often shared similar views and understood similar plights; they were after all both coming from peoples affected by communism.

In May 2001, in what could be retrospectively construed as a prophetic move the late Pontiff extended an olive branch to the Muslim world. It was while on a visit to Syria Pope John Paul II became the first Catholic Pontiff to visit a Mosque in Islam's 1,400-year history. The purpose of the visit was to try and bridge the gap between Christianity and Islam. Ironically his pilgrimage would take place just months before September 11th and was done with a view to try and warn the Islamic world and all religions about the dangers of fundamentalism.

The Pope used the occasion to urge Christians and Muslims to forgive each other for the past, speaking inside the Great Umayyad Mosque, a splendid testimonial to Syrian history, the weary-looking Pontiff said religious conviction was never a justification for violence.

"Nevermore communities in conflict," he told Muslim leaders who included the Grand Mufti of Syria. Outside lays the tomb of Saladin, who drove the Crusaders from the East. The Pontiff said it was now time to turn the page with Islam too.

For all the times that Muslims and Christians have offended one another, we need to seek forgiveness from the Almighty and to offer each other forgiveness," he said in his address.

"Better mutual understanding will surely lead... to a new way of presenting our two religions, not in opposition as has happened too often in the past, but in partnership for the good of the human family."

The theme of the Pontiff's visit was mutual forgiveness, expressed days before in Greece, where he sought God's pardon for the wrongs committed by Catholics against the Orthodox faithful in the past 1,000 years. Then, a few days later in the Mosque there was a clear sense that history was being made as the Pope, helped by an Arabic interpreter, spoke offering a pressing appeal against religious fundamentalism from any side.

"It is crucial for the young to be taught the ways of respect and understanding, so they will not be led to misuse religion itself to promote or justify hatred and violence." Violence destroys the image of the Creator and should never be considered as the fruit of religious conviction."

Indeed, a strong desire for unity in the world was one of the reasons why Faustina's writings were so important to Pope John Paul II. The Pontiff believed that the messages contained in her Diary were of universal appeal. He also reminded us when he revealed the third secret of Fatima that throughout history there have been supernatural apparitions and signs which go to the heart of human events and which, to the surprise of believers and non-believers alike, play their part in the unfolding of history.

The Pope sincerely believed the same philosophy could be applied to Faustina's Diary. He was a man who cared deeply about humanity and would use every opportunity to voice his concern. However, Pope John Paul II's greatest plea was that all mankind know the image and the messages because he was absolutely convinced Faustina's words came from Christ, and were meant to be shared with the entire human family. The Pontiff also realized the messages had a proven track record and had given great hope to the nation of Poland. In fact until the Vatican ban was imposed, devotion to The Divine Mercy and The Image spread like a flood throughout Poland and gave great comfort to that nation during the War. Also given the Pope's Polish background, his theological expertise, and great intelligence, he was able to understand The Diary better than most people. The Pope knew that all the apparitions of the 20th century had involved sightings of the Virgin Mary. The apparitions Faustina received on the other hand came from Christ.

The Pope also grew up in the same political climate as Faustina and shared a great spirituality with her. Some have also described Pope John Paul II as a great mystic, an ability which he shared not only with Faustina but also with some of his predecessors.

Just how mystical Pope John Paul II was is known only to God but he clearly had a positive effect on all he met and at times seemed to achieve the impossible. This was of course most evident in his role in the fall of Eastern Block Communism. Yet it is difficult to fully understand the apparitions and visions that he received because signs given to the successors of Peter are often kept secret for a variety of reasons. Firstly members of the Vatican's hierarchy do not like to broadcast the mystical experiences of the head of the Catholic Church. From time to time details of such incidents do surface, but these are given almost always without attribution and as a result, these episodes are nearly impossible to independently follow-up and evaluate.

If however, Pope John Paul was a visionary he was not the only Pontiff to have encountered such experiences.

Just under a century before Pope John Paul II's Pontificate, on October 13, 1884 there was an instance involving Leo XIII. As the story is recounted it was shortly after completing a celebration of Mass in one of the Vatican's private chapels when the Pontiff while standing at the foot of the altar, suddenly turned ashen and collapsed to the floor. To those present, the Pope appeared to have been an apparent victim of a stroke or heart attack. However, neither malady was the cause of his collapse. Instead according to testimony he had been given a vision of the future of the Church he loved so much. Then after a few minutes spent in what seemed like a coma, he revived and remarked to those around him, "Oh, what a horrible picture I was permitted to see!"

What Leo XIII apparently saw, as described later by those who talked to him was a period of about one hundred years when the power of Satan would reach its zenith. That period was to be the twentieth century. Leo was so shaken by the specter of the destruction of moral and spiritual values both inside and outside the Church, that he was prompted to compose a prayer which was to be said at the end of each Mass celebrated anywhere in the Catholic Church. This prayer to Michael the Archangel was said continuously until the Mass was restructured in the Second Vatican council. The prayer is as follows:

> *Saint Michael the Archangel, defend us in battle; be our defense against the wickedness and snares of the devil. May God rebuke him, we humbly pray; and do you, O Prince of the heavenly host, by the power of God, thrust into hell Satan and the other evil spirits who prowl about the world for the ruin of souls. Amen.*

It should be noted that virtually all measures of social pathology and moral decline (things like the crime rate, percentage of unwed mothers, abortion rate, divorce rate, etc.) started to rise sharply as the 1960's ended and at a time when this prayer had ceased being used in Church liturgies. Regardless, while the precise details of Leo's visions are not known, it would certainly appear that his concerns about the coming difficulties in his Church and the world in which it found itself were well founded.

There were also occasional rumors of visions and "angelic" phenomena associated with Pius XII during the entire duration of his papacy (1939 - 1958). He purportedly experienced mystical visions of both Jesus and Mary. After one of these "visions" he reportedly told an assistant, "Mankind must prepare itself for sufferings such as it has never before experienced."

To reaffirm the trust he exhibited in the Mother of God, Pope Pius X11 also witnessed the inexplicable solar phenomena of Fatima while walking in the Vatican gardens. It was an experience he wrote about to one of his cardinals,

"Having lifted the papers I had in my hand, I was struck by a phenomenon I had never seen before. The sun, which was fairly high, looked like a pale yellow opaque globe completely surrounded by a luminous halo, which nevertheless did not prevent me at all from staring attentively at the sun without the slightest discomfort. A very light cloud was before it. The opaque globe began moving outward, slowly turning over upon itself, and going from left to right and vice-versa. But within the globe very strong movements could be seen in all clarity and without interruption.

So great was his belief in this vision, two days after these experiences in the Vatican garden Pius XII formally declared as Catholic Dogma that Mary was assumed body and soul into Heaven - a doctrine known now as the Assumption and a Feast day was installed.

Pope John Paul II's vision also involved Fatima. It was on May 13, 1981, during an open-air papal audience in St. Peter's Square, the Polish Pope who had dedicated his papacy to Mary, bent down to hug a young girl who was wearing a small likeness of Our Lady of Fatima. At that precise moment, Mehmet Ali Agca, a Turkish assassin, fired shots at his head at close range. It was at about 1715 local time, the Pope, being driven in his Pope mobile through a crowd of about 20,000 worshippers was shot with bullets from a 9mm pistol some 15 feet away. Two of the bullets struck him in the stomach, one in his right arm and the fourth hit his little finger.

Had John Paul II not bent down to hug that little girl wearing the picture of Mary, those bullets might have ripped through his skull probably killing him instantly. The events of that day were indeed truly miraculous. Writer Andre Frossard has described the sequence of events that followed as without a doubt miraculous.

Firstly the would-be assassin assumed the Pope was wearing a bulletproof vest: this is why he did not aim for the heart, but at the stomach instead. The Pope moved his hand at the moment the assassin fired; the bullet struck his finger and changed its course by a millimeter, and because of this it missed an artery. Had it struck the artery, he would have bled to death in minutes. As author Pawel Zuchniewicz recalls Frossards account of the story in his bestseller "*Miracles of John Paul II*," after two shots Ali Acga's gun jammed. They drove the Pope to the ambulance that he had blessed the day before, saying, "May it never be needed." The ambulance had been donated to the Vatican and was kept nearby in case a pilgrim needed assistance. It reached the Gemelli clinic in eight minutes, even though it usually takes forty minutes given the traffic at that time of day. What was even more amazing according to Frossard is that they got there so fast without a siren; it had broken down. Then of course, there was the operation. The clinic personnel were waiting for the Pope knowing that something had happened but they didn't know what. It could have been a heart attack, a stroke, or some kind of accident. Worse yet, the most experienced surgeon, Professor Francesco Crucitti, was not there nor was he at home. There were no cellular phones in those days.

In fact, Professor Crucitti had been visiting a patient elsewhere and suddenly looked up to see a very distraught nun in the doorway at the clinic on Rome's via Aurelia.

"Professor! The Holy Father!" she cried out. "There was an attempt on his life! They shot him!"

Crucitti stared at her stunned. "No this is impossible!" he thought. "Where is the phone?" he asked.

The sister took him to the phone. The professor dialed the number to the Gemelli. One, two, three rings…Nobody was answering! He quickly changed and put on his jacket. In no time at all he was in the car. Traffic jams! Rome's traffic jams! Crucitti decided on a make or break maneuver. He got in the left lane, put his hand on the horn, and joined a convoy of speeding cars with their sirens blaring. A moment later he saw a policeman on a motorcycle chasing him. When the policeman pulled up by the car, the professor yelled out in desperation, "I have to be at Gemelli immediately!"

The policeman understood. He sped up and made way for Crucitti. Within a few minutes they were at the entrance of the hospital. In the operating room the team literally tore off Crucitti's clothes. In a few seconds he had his operation uniform on. He washed his hands as they put on his overall and his shoes. The doctor came in. "Pressure 80, 70 and falling," he said. They entered the room. Dr. Crucitti leaned over the Pope. He saw blood—a lot of blood. They began to drain the abdominal cavity. After a moment they were able to see the damage. Dr. Crucitti stopped the bleeding. Crucitti saw many wounds in the abdominal cavity. One was created by the bullet, the other by bursting. The worst injury was at the rear of the colon. However, no vital organ had been disturbed: the bullet only brushed the organs that if damaged could have meant death. A half-hour before midnight the last stitches were put in and on May 14, at 12.45 am, a statement was issued that the operation had been a success.

"When I fell in St Peter's Square I had a distinct feeling that I would recover," said the Pope to Andre Frossard, "the bullet as he was showing me the film, momentarily changed direction as of it came up against a piece of steel. This is unthinkable because inside the body the parts are soft; there aren't any bones. How this happened only our most Blessed Virgin Mary knows." Indeed without this miraculous event the world would have been deprived of a great Pope and there may not have been the canonization of Saint Faustina.

As it was, it would take John Paul II six months to fully recover from the wounds and as he convalesced at the Policlinico in Rome, he became even more prayerful and believed Our Lady of Fatima's direct intercession had saved his life. He reread the three Secrets that the Lady of Fatima gave the three children in 1917 and which were finally recorded in written form by one of the children who would later became Sister Lucia. Pope John Paul II then instructed Bishop Pavol Hnilica, a Slovak bishop who was secretly ordained while a priest in communist Czechoslovakia, to send all the Church's documents on the events at Fatima for his review. The Pope also dispatched Sister Mary Ludovica to Fatima to meet with its retired Bishop John Venancio. The purpose of this meeting was never disclosed.

It was while he was in this state of mind at the Policlinico that John Paul reportedly witnessed the inexplicable phenomenon of the sun first seen at Fatima sixty five years earlier. At that moment, he reportedly received a vision of the future related to the third Fatima Secret.

What were the contents of his vision? Only John Paul knows. However, Bishop Hnilica reported that at the time of the Pope's release from the Policlinico, the Pope told him: "I have come to understand that the only way to save the world from war, to save it from atheism, is the conversion of Russia according to the message of Fatima." It is reasonable to suspect that, since the time of this vision, the Pope began acting in accord with what he believed were Heaven's wishes.

John Paul II, had already dedicated his papacy to Mary, the Mother of Jesus and some believe he was in constant mental prayer to her throughout his life. The Pope's personal motto was Totus Tuus (Completely Yours), a term illustrating the consecration of his life to the Blessed Virgin, a consecration that took place while he was still a Polish bishop or even, possibly when he became a motherless child?

The assassination attempt and the vision that followed it serve to affirm Mary's unique role for Pope John Paul II. He called the assassination attempt a "mysterious coincidence with the anniversary of the first apparition at Fatima" in a speech he gave as a pilgrim to Fatima on May 13, 1982. During this pilgrimage, John Paul also conducted a service where he consecrated the world and, indirectly, Russia, to the Immaculate Heart of Mary. His actions following his recovery suggested that he began operating on a timetable established by Heaven and it is certain that both Fatima and Faustina played a major role.

It was obvious the role of the Virgin Mother reigned supreme for the Pope yet it is evident that Faustina's role as Christ secretary was a pivotal one for his Papacy, and it is interesting the two women who helped form the basis of his time as successor to Peter were the Mother of God, and Saint Faustina.

Could it be his mysticism that made him arrive at his complete trust in Faustina's messages? Certainly as Pope he was capable of extraordinary accomplishments.

Indeed, it may not be surprising that various Popes have received visions when we consider the actual meaning of the word Vatican. Research the word *Vatican* in many Latin - English / English - Latin dictionaries, or encyclopedias, and you will likely find that Vatican City and St. Peter's Basilica of the Roman Catholic Church were built upon what was called in Latin *vaticanus mons* or *vaticanus collies*. The words *mons* and *collis* mean hill or mountain. You will also find in the dictionaries that the words vatic / vates / vatis all relate to prophecy.

Vaticanus then is a combination of Vatic + anus, just as Romanus is a combination of Rome + anus. Therefore, vaticanus collis or vaticanus mons means *"the prophetic hill or mountain,"* which can be rephrased as *the hill or mountain of prophecy.*

The word Vatican actually derives from the Latin *vates*, which means "tellers of the future." This name was the name given to a hillside on the west bank of the Tiber River in Rome because daily lineups of fortunetellers used to hawk their "wares" to passersby on the street. Many Popes who have had visions or mystical powers have gone on to become saints, which may be the case with Pope John Paul II. Following his death, a number of clergy at the Vatican and laymen throughout the world have been referring to the late pontiff as "John Paul the Great"— only the fourth pope to be so acclaimed and the first since the first millennium.

Pope Benedict XVI, his successor, referred to him as "the great Pope John Paul II" in his first address from the loggia of St Peter's Church. While still Cardinal Ratzinger, he had stirred excitement when in his published written homily for the Mass of Repose, he referred to John Paul II as "the Great." Since then Benedict has continued to refer to John Paul II as "the Great". At the 2005 World Youth Day in Germany, speaking in Polish, John Paul's native language, Benedict said, "As the great Pope John Paul II would say: keep the flame of faith alive in your lives and your people."

In fact, scholars of Canon Law say that there is no official process for declaring a pope "Great"; the title establishes itself through popular, and continued, usage. The three popes who today commonly are known as "Great" are Leo I, who reigned from 440-461 and persuaded Attila the Hun to withdraw from Rome, thus saving Christianity and Catholicism in Europe from destruction; Gregory 1, 590-604, after whom the Gregorian Chant is named; and Nicholas 1 858-867, who also withstood a siege of Rome. (in this case from *Carolingian Christians, over a dispute regarding marriage annulment*).

Then in a move that could make the title official on 9 May 2005 Benedict XVI began the beatification process for his predecessor. Normally five years must pass after a person's death before the beatification process can begin. However, in an audience with Pope Benedict XVI, Camillo Cardinal Ruini cited "exceptional circumstances" which suggested the waiting period could be waived. As Vicar General of the Diocese of Rome, Ruini is the person responsible for promoting the cause for canonization of any person who dies within that diocese. (In all other dioceses it would be the Bishop himself.) The "exceptional circumstances" presumably refer to the People's cries of "Santo Subito!" ("Saint now") during the late pontiff's funeral. Therefore the new Pope waived the five year rule "so that the cause of Beatification and Canonization of the same Servant of God can begin immediately." The decision was announced on 13 May 2005, the Feast of Our Lady of Fatima and the 24th anniversary of the murder attempt on John Paul II in St Peter's Square. Cardinal Ruini inaugurated the diocesan phase of the cause for beatification in the Lateran Basilica on 28 June 2005.

In early 2006, the process began to speed up when it was reported that the Vatican was investigating a possible miracle attributed to the late Pontiff. The investigation involves a French nun, who though confined to her bed with Parkinson's disease, is reported to have experienced a "complete and lasting cure after members of her community prayed for the intercession of Pope John Paul II."

On May 28, 2006, Pope Benedict XVI while saying Mass before an estimated 900,000 people in John Paul II's native Poland asked the congregation to pray for the early canonization of John Paul II and stated that he hoped canonization would happen "in the near future."

This possibility became even more likely when in Nov, 2006, an Italian bishop claimed Pope John Paul II miraculously cured a man of lung cancer after his wife prayed to the late pontiff.

Gerardo Pierro, the archbishop of Salerno, said that John Paul appeared to the wife in a dream to tell her that her husband would recover. A few weeks later doctors pronounced the cancer completely gone, he said.

Indeed, Pope Benedict XVI has already put John Paul on the fast track for beatification, the first stage in the process of becoming a saint. To be beatified, a candidate must have led an exemplary life, demonstrated heroic virtue and been responsible for at least one miracle, generally a medically inexplicable cure. The reported cancer cure could be the second miracle needed for canonization.

Therefore, we have a Pope with extraordinary gifts who took Faustina seriously enough to make her a Saint and who would within five years of that canonization be considered for Sainthood himself. Was this all part of his unique concern for humanity along with his apparent concern to work on heaven's time table?

What is known is that he was very much aware of the places Faustina mentioned, the life she described and also knew that much of what she had predicted had in fact come true.

It is in light of Pope John Paul II's understanding of Faustina's visions, apparitions, writings and his belief that Faustina's future prophecies would soon transpire that he felt compelled to share them with the world and catapult her to Sainthood.

Yet even as Pontiff, Pope John Paul II knew declaring a mystic a Saint based solely on the messages found in her Diary would not be plausible. Instead, it would require miracles of a medical nature to make this happen.

Pope John Paul II was of course no stranger to medical miracles. After being shot by Mehmet Ali Agca and as surgeons performed a five-hour operation, the world prayed. There was a distinct chance the world would lose a Pope to assassination. Miraculously however the prayers were answered.

Now Pope John Paul II, having had his own life saved was determined to bring his reinforced faith to the rest of humanity. It was a faith given by God and subsequently made stronger by the messages of hope in *The Diary*. The Pope now needed miracles in order to canonize Faustina and would start praying for them. Hardly surprising just as with all his prayers to his spiritual friend, Sister Faustina Kowalska, Pope John Paul II's prayers would soon be answered!

CHAPTER TWELVE

MIRACLES CAN HAPPEN

The universe in which man lives is not limited to the order that can be ascertained through logic or senses. A Miracle is a "sign" that the order we perceive is superseded by a "Power from above."

—John Paul II General Audience, January 1988

Very few outside of the Catholic Church are aware of the fascinating and very involved process by which a person becomes a saint. The road to sainthood, while entailing a very thorough and even scientific investigation, actually begins at the grassroots. It is most-often local and ordinary people who, having been particularly inspired by an extraordinarily holy individual, eventually petition a local bishop to consider such for investigation with the hope that they may one day become recognized as a saint. This process of becoming a saint is called canonization. However, before canonization is ever achieved, the first step in the process is called *beatification.*

Beatification is more of a localized recognition by the Church of a saint, while canonization brings a universal recognition throughout the Church. This process begins with a request to a local bishop. If the bishop sees merit in the request, he will set up a board of experts to investigate the individual being nominated for sainthood. The individual's life, their faith, and their reputation for holiness will all become the subject of a thorough investigation. Surviving family members, acquaintances, and colleagues will all be interviewed. Any miraculous events associated with that person's life will be examined by a panel of medical experts and theologians. If, after this initial investigation, the nominee is found to pass all of these requirements, then the bishop may choose to petition Rome to begin the process of beatification. The full investigation until that point is compiled into a report and submitted to the Vatican's Congregation for the Causes of Saints—a group of theological experts and cardinals.

If after this thorough review, The Congregation finds the candidate's life to have been truly heroic, the Pope can bless the candidate and veneration may be offered by the local church.

The process of assessing Faustina's life, her exercise of heroic virtues, her writings, and her devotions began on Oct. 21, 1965. But beyond this first investigative step, there must also have been at least one authenticating miracle (usually a physical healing) after the death of the candidate, and one which must be proven through the scrutiny of a body of medical experts. The healings must be instant and irreversible. If such a miracle or miracles are found to have occurred by the panel, then the Pope may bless the candidate and allow for a local veneration of the blessed individual. The candidate has been *beatified*.

Faustina's first miracle was to have occurred in March of 1981 when Maureen Digan, of Roslindale, Massachusetts, her husband, son, and Fr. Seraphim Michalenko, traveled to Faustina's tomb at the Shrine of The Divine Mercy outside of Krakow, Poland. From her early teens, Maureen suffered from Milroy's Disease, an incurable form of lymphedema. Maureen had all but given up hope that she would ever be free from this disease, which had already claimed one of her legs, and doctors were recommending that the other be amputated as well. Upon arriving at Faustina's tomb, Maureen prayed for Faustina's intercession. It was at that moment that Maureen immediately felt the pain leave her body and watched as the swelling in her leg went away. It was such a supernatural shock that Maureen later admitted that she thought she was losing her mind. However, upon a complete examination by her doctors, it was declared that Maureen's incurable disease had completely disappeared. Then, after an exhaustive examination by medical professionals, the Church declared the healing a miracle through Faustina's intercession. It was on April 18, 1993 that St. Faustina was beatified by Pope John Paul II at the Vatican.

The final step beyond beatification is canonization. The canonization process involves the blessing of the Pope to venerate and honor the Saint throughout the entire Catholic Church. In order to be canonized, it is necessary that a second miracle wrought through prayer be validated. In Faustina's case this occurred in 1995 in Baltimore Maryland.

At 48, Father Ron Pytel knew that he had a serious problem. During a bout with bronchitis, he found himself out of breath after climbing a flight of stairs. After an examination, the doctors revealed to Fr. Pytel that his condition was indeed serious. A massive calcium build-up was significantly blocking his aortic valve. As a result of the blockage, Fr. Patel's heart had also become badly damaged—a condition that rarely heals and if it does, it occurs over a span of many years.

In June of 1995, Fr. Ron had surgery to replace this damaged aortic valve with an artificial one, but the damage to his heart was another problem. When he went for his first regular check-up two months later, the prognosis was not good. Dr. Nicholas Fortuin, a world-renowned cardiologist from Johns Hopkins in Baltimore, said that Fr. Ron's heart would never be normal and that he would likely never be able to return to his priestly duties.

However, all of that changed on Oct. 5, 1995—the Feast Day and 58th anniversary of Faustina's death. After a full day of prayer at his parish, Fr. Ron attended a healing service where he prayed for Faustina's intercession. After venerating her relic, he collapsed on the floor and felt unable to move for about 15 minutes. During his next regular check-up, Fr. Ron's doctor could not explain the condition of the priest's heart — it had returned to normal.

Soon after his healing, Fr. Pytel contacted Fr. Seraphim Michalenko, who had accompanied Maureen Digan to Poland several years earlier when she experienced her miraculous healing at Faustina's tomb. Father Seraphim was also the representative for North America in furthering Faustina's cause of canonization. Father Seraphim then began to work with church authorities in gathering the documentation of Fr. Pytel's healing as the miracle needed for Faustina's canonization. This healing, like all presented to the Church as "miracles," was thoroughly and exhaustively researched by medical professionals and theologians who deal with the causes for saints.

On November 16th and December 9th, 1999, respective teams of medical and theological experts at the Vatican concluded their definitive investigation of Fr. Pytel's healing. The medical professional representing the Postulators of Faustina's cause was Dr. Valentin Fuster, Director of Mt. Sinai's Cardiovascular Institute in New York City. He is regarded as the preeminent expert in the world in the field of cardiovascular disease.

The medical doctors evaluated the healing as scientifically unexplainable, and the theologians attributed it to the intercession of Saint Faustina. The healing was declared a miracle by theologians from the Church's Congregation for the Causes of Saints on Dec. 7. One week later, on Dec. 14, a panel of cardinals and bishops gave their unanimous approval. Finally, the solemn promulgation of the decree declaring the healing a miracle took place at the Vatican in the presence of Pope John Paul II on Dec. 20, 1999.

In his book *the miracles of John Paul II*" bestselling Polish author Pawel Zuchniewicz writes about another miracle of Saint Faustina. Though not used to proclaim her canonization this story nonetheless confirms the miraculous powers of the Image and the value of prayer in the presence of the image. In the chapter "pray to my sister Faustina," the author tells the story of a young man whose faith was restored via the Image of Divine Mercy. A man who had every reason to give up on life, Ugo Festa was a man who lived with great suffering. Plagued with Multiple sclerosis, muscular dystrophy, and epilepsy Ugo also had serious difficulties with both his eyesight and spinal cord. Born in Vicenza, Italy, in 1951 the realization that he would never be well had accompanied him since childhood. At times this had created in Ugo a lack of trust in any higher power and especially in the existence of God.

On one occasion while hospitalized another patient upon witnessing Ugo's great despair and apparent lack of faith suggested that he take a pilgrimage to Lourdes. Believing the sight of Bernadette's apparitions to be nothing but superstition he reluctantly agreed to go. Once there according to Zuchniewicz, "He experienced something surprising. He was not healed, but gained the conviction that God does indeed exist."

Some years later another transformation occurred when Ugo went on a pilgrimage to Rome for the beatification of Fr. Filipo Rinaldi. Ugo arrived in Rome on April 28th 1990 and was overjoyed to be introduced to Mother Teresa of Calcutta. Mother Teresa bent down and gave Ugo a hug. Then one of her sisters invited Ugo to go to a retreat with them. He said that he would stay in Rome. "At least take this," said the sister presenting him with a miraculous medal and some pictures from her bag. Ugo looked at the image, and the sister explained that it was the Image of Divine Mercy. Then they parted ways.

The next day according to Zuchniewicz; "Ugo was in St Peter's square with other sick people waiting for the Pope, who traditionally stopped by those seated in wheelchairs. Seeing John Paul II, Ugo extended to him the images and medallion he had received.

"Holy Father, bless them," he begged.

The Holy Father made the sign of the cross over the items and bent down over Ugo.

"How do you feel?" the Holy Father asked him.

"Terrible. I am living through a terrible crisis."

How can you say that while holding an Image of the Divine Mercy in your hand?" the Pope asked him, smiling lightly. "Entrust yourself to Him and pray to my Sister Faustina asking for her intercession."

Watching the figure of the Pope dressed in white as he walked away, Ugo recalled the sisters' invitation to the retreat at Trent from the sister the day before. 'Maybe I should go," he thought. He went that same year.

For three days Ugo sat before a reproduction of the Divine Mercy Image, the Image that Faustina was commissioned to have painted in Trent. On the fourth day he returned. He sat in his wheelchair and gazed. All of a sudden there was a twitch in his body and he felt warmth passing through him. Upon hearing the words Jesus came towards him "Get up and walk" he understood at that moment he was completely well. He walked out of the church. There was not a single trace of his illness left. Ugo became convinced that it was God himself who had invited him. After all, he had initially said 'no' to Mother Teresa's nun and only the words of Pope John Paul II changed his mind. Ugo went back to Rome and during a general audience got to tell this to the Pope himself. He then went to India to work with Mother Teresa's nuns, and later went to Africa to work among the poor there. Upon his return to Italy he organized a hospice in his hometown for the neediest among his own community. In

2005 Ugo learned he had cancer, but he was not devastated "What should I worry about? Jesus saved me once, so everything will be fine again."

Though he wasn't healed, it was not the cancer that took his life. On May 22, 2005, he was found in a pool of blood, his head torn apart by bullets from a revolver. A week later, two individuals were arrested on Murder charges. As Pawet Zuchniewicz reminds us "Ugo Festa lived only a month and a half longer than the man who fifteen years earlier told him to entrust himself to Divine Mercy." Yet he lived those last years as a man healed of his sufferings and with a trust developed because he was told to pray to Saint Faustina.

In *Faustina's Diary*, Saint Faustina recounts her mystical experiences, including Christ's declaration that she was His Secretary and the Apostle of His Mercy. His urgent message is that mankind shall not have peace until it turns with trust to His mercy. Now, 62 years after her death, Faustina was well on her way to making *The Image* and the messages of *Christ's Divine Mercy* known to the world. Though Faustina is no longer alive it is evident that through prayers, miracles were received, and her mission continues. It was just as Christ had told her and as she recorded In *The Diary*, "I have chosen you for that office in this life and the next."

CHAPTER THIRTEEN

MISUNDERSTOOD SOUL BECOMES A SAINT

During his distinguished Papacy, Pope John Paul II canonized more Saints than any other Pope in history. Yet there was one ceremony that stood out beyond the others and with very good reason.

Though known by many Catholics as "the Great Mercy Pope," Pope John Paul II was spiritually connected to Faustina in a way that many could not understand. He felt that he was also part of the plan that God had entrusted to her.

John Paul would die on *the Vigil of the Feast of the Divine Mercy* a celebration which he inaugurated on April 30, 2000 because of instructions written in *Faustina's Diary*. They were directives from Christ to install this Feast day back into the Church after it had been omitted for centuries. The reintroduction of this Feast was not only to be the day that the Pope proclaimed Faustina as a Saint, but was also an occasion which he described as "the happiest day of his life." It seems somewhat strange, considering all the other holy men and women that The Pope elevated to the position of Sainthood, that this day would be so significant for him. Why did Faustina's proclamation of Sainthood cause him the most joy? Could it be that in proclaiming Faustina's Sainthood, he was bringing the world to a greater awareness of *The Diary* and the messages contained within its six hundred pages? After all, these other candidates had met the necessary criteria for canonization but none of them had a message which formed the basis of this Pope's entire pontificate, nor had they provided the Pope with his "Special mission on earth." They also never had a special celebration reinstated in the Church that dealt with man's salvation!

It was on November 22, 1981— the Feast of Christ the King—when Pope John Paul II made his first public appearance outside of Rome since the attempt on his life. He visited the Shrine of Merciful Love in Collevalenza near Todi, Italy. Within a few days, an international congress was to be held to reflect on the Encyclical *Dives in Misericordia (Rich in Mercy)* one year after its publication. After celebrating the Holy Sacrifice of the Eucharist, he made a strong public declaration about the importance of the message of mercy:

"A year ago I published the encyclical Dives in Misericordia. This circumstance made me come to the Sanctuary of Merciful Love today. By my presence I wish to reconfirm, in a way, the message of that encyclical. I wish to read it again and deliver it again. Right from the beginning of my ministry in St. Peter's See in Rome, I considered this message my special task. Providence has assigned it to me in the present situation of man, the Church, and the world. It could be said that precisely this situation assigned that message to me as my task before God."

On April 6, 1986, which would later become Divine Mercy Sunday the Pope further emphasized his commitment to Christ's messages through Faustina while addressing pilgrims in St. Peter's Square, Rome at the noonday recitation of the Regina Caeli:

"I direct now my affectionate greeting to all the groups of pilgrims present in St. Peter's Square; in particular, I express a cordial welcome to the group of Roman supporters of The Divine Mercy according to the message of Sr. Faustina Kowalska who celebrate today the feast of The Divine Mercy."

Then on April 10, 1991 during the Easter message of the merciful Christ at his General audience, Pope John Paul II again spoke about Sister Faustina, showing his great respect for her, relating her to his encyclical, *Rich in Mercy,* and emphasizing her role in bringing the message of mercy to the world: (*L'Osservatore Romano*, April 15, 1991)

> *"We pray for this through the intercession of her who*
> *does not cease to proclaim 'mercy... from generation to*
> *generation,' and also through the intercession of those for*

whom there have been completely fulfilled the words of
the Sermon on the Mount: 'Blessed are the merciful, for
they shall obtain mercy.'

— Dives in Misericordia, 15

The words of the encyclical on Divine Mercy (Dives in Misericordia) are particularly close to us. They recall the figure of the Servant of God, Sister Faustina Kowalska. This simple religious woman particularly brought the Easter message of the merciful Christ closer to Poland and the whole world. This happened before the Second World War with all its cruelty. In the face of all the organized contempt for the human person, the message of Christ who was tormented and rose again became for many people in Poland and beyond its borders, and even on other continents, a source of the hope and strength necessary for survival.

In addition, today? Is it perhaps not necessary also "in the contemporary world" in our homeland, in society, among the people who have entered into a new phase of our history, for love to reveal that it is stronger than hatred and selfishness? Is it perhaps not necessary to translate into the language of today's generations the words of the Gospel, "blessed are the merciful, for they shall obtain mercy" (Mt 5:7)?

O Mother, who announces divine mercy "from generation to generation" (Lk 1:50), help our generation to rise from the moral crisis. May Christ's new commandment, "love one another" (Jn 13:34) be established ever more fully among us."

On Sunday, April 18, 1993 Pope John Paul II's love for Sister Faustina was evident once again as he beatified her in St. Peter's Square, Vatican City. Even though this was only the first step towards canonization, her popularity was clearly growing, and at the Mass to celebrate the occasion there were over 100,000 pilgrims from all over the world. John Paul preached the homily in Italian, Spanish, Polish, saluting Faustina and the great gifts she gave to the world.

"*I salute you, Sister Faustina.* Beginning today the Church calls you Blessed, especially the Church in Poland and Lithuania. O Faustina, how extraordinary your life is! Precisely you, the poor and simple daughter of Mazovia, of the Polish people, chosen by Christ to remind people of this great mystery of Divine Mercy! You bore this mystery within yourself, leaving this world after a short life, filled with suffering. However, at the same time, this mystery has become a prophetic reminder to the world, to Europe. Your message of Divine Mercy was born almost on the eve of World War II. Certainly you would have been amazed if you could have experienced upon this earth what this message meant for the suffering people during that hour of torment, and how it spread throughout the world. Today, we truly believe, you contemplate in God the fruits of your mission on earth. Today you experience it at its very source, which is your Christ…

"I clearly feel that my mission does not end with death, but begins," Sister Faustina wrote in her *Diary*. Moreover, it truly did! Her mission continues and is yielding astonishing fruit. It is truly marvelous how her devotion to the merciful Jesus is spreading in our contemporary world and gaining so many human hearts! This is doubtlessly a *sign of the times* — a *sign of our 20th century*. The balance of this century which is now ending, in addition to the advances which have often surpassed those of preceding eras, presents a deep restlessness and fear of the future. Where, if not in *The Divine Mercy*, can the world find refuge and the light of hope? Believers understand that perfectly… "Give thanks to the Lord, for He is good. Give thanks to the Lord, for He is merciful." Today, on the day of the Beatification of Sister Faustina, we praise the Lord for the great things He has done in her soul, we praise and thank Him for the great things He has done and always continues to do in the souls who through Sister Faustina's witness and message discover the infinite depths of *The Divine Mercy*."

The next day, back in St Peter's Square, The Pope addressed Faustina's religious community and again spoke of the importance of the messages.

"May this mystery be for every one of you the inspiration and the strength to carry out the divine mercy in actual life. In the name of this mystery, Christ teaches us to pardon always and to love one another reciprocally as He himself has loved us. Since we came back to Sr. Faustina, one more wish, that these simple words, "Jesus, I trust in You!" that I see here on so many images, continually be for human hearts also in the future, near the end of this century and this millennium, and the next, a clear indicator of the way."

Clearly, Faustina's message and *The Image* were of vital importance to the late Holy Father. In recounting the statements that he made about her, we are given some indication of why he singled out her canonization ceremony as one that gave him so much happiness. After all, each Saint was elevated on their own merit and had been able to meet all the requirements of heroic virtue and certainly passed the litmus test of the so called "devil's advocate."

There were indeed many lengthy and thorough investigations in order to perform each and every one of the canonization ceremonies by Pope John Paul II. He proclaimed more saints during his papacy than any other pontiff. In fact according to the Vatican archives he gave an extraordinary impetus to Canonizations and Beatifications, focusing on countless examples of holiness as an incentive for the people of our time. John Paul celebrated 147 beatification ceremonies during which he proclaimed 1,338 Blesseds; and 51 canonizations for a total of 482 saints. Yet his comments at Saint Faustina's canonization suggest there was something far more significant about this woman—something which separated her heroic value from all the others who were canonized.

For while each canonization caused tremendous joy to the pope Faustina's ceremony was different—especially for Pope John Paul II. Firstly John Paul was well aware that the occasion provided further confirmation of Faustina's prophetic ability; it was after all an occasion that she had perfectly described in her *Diary* written some sixty years earlier. It is also interesting to note that while many of the lives of other Saints had fulfilled important tasks during their lifetimes, Saint Faustina's task concerned the future. Her mission was to bring mankind's attention to the messages that Christ imparted to her, which could only be achieved after her death. This canonization ceremony confirmed the Church's belief that the messages were indeed authentically sent from God and John Paul could now sanction them and share them with the world.

Now with a capacity crowd witnessing the proclamation of her Sainthood, the world was starting to pay attention to this woman and her messages from Christ.

It was at the crack of dawn—the time when the Basilica of St Peter's is at its most glorious—that the crowds started pouring into the Piazza. They arrived in the thousands in what would be one of the largest crowd ever witnessed at a canonization ceremony. An estimated 250,000 pilgrims gathered in St. Peter's that day to celebrate her Sainthood. It was a celebration which she had foreseen and written of in her Diary entry 1044.

"Suddenly God's presence took hold of me, and at once I saw myself in Rome, in the Holy Father's chapel and at the same time I was in Chapel. In addition, at the celebration of the Holy Father and the entire Church was closely linked to our chapel and, in a special way, with our congregation. And I took part in the solemn celebration simultaneously here and in Rome, for the celebration was closely connected to Rome that, even as I write, I can not distinguish the two but I am writing it down as I saw it."

What is interesting about this prophecy is Faustina's description of a simultaneous event. In fact, on the occasion of her canonization, television screens beamed live images from Rome to her convent in Krakow where 300,000 worshipers had gathered at her convent to watch the ceremony live from Rome.

This quite well describes Faustina's vision, though when Faustina was alive, Television was of course not yet available. Perhaps only Divine inspiration can explain how she was able to write of an event fifty-two years before it happened and to see technology that had not yet been invented.

As Faustina further describes:

"I saw the Lord Jesus in our chapel, exposed in the Monstrance on the high altar. The chapel was adorned for the feast, and on that day anyone who wanted to come was allowed in. The crowd was so enormous that the eye could not take it in. Everyone was participating in the celebrations with great joy, and many of them obtained what they desired. The same celebration was held in Rome, in a beautiful church, and the Holy Father, with all the clergy, was celebrating the feast, and then suddenly I saw Saint Peter, who stood between the altar and the Holy Father. I could not hear what Saint Peter said but I saw the Holy Father understood his words..."

Indeed, from the smile on Pope John Paul's face that day, it seemed that he believed he was carrying out God's plan. It was also evident from the words he spoke:

Today my joy is truly great in presenting the life and witness of Sr. Faustina Kowalska to the whole Church as a gift of God for our time. By Divine Providence, the life of this humble daughter of Poland was completely linked with the history of the 20th century, the century we have just left behind. In fact, it was between the First and Second World Wars that Christ entrusted His message of mercy to her. Those who remember, who were witnesses and participants in the events of those years and the horrible sufferings they caused for millions of people, know well how necessary was the message of mercy. Jesus told Sr. Faustina: "Humanity will not find peace until it turns trustfully to divine mercy" (*Diary* entry 300). Through the work of the Polish religious, this message has become linked forever to the 20th century, the last of the second millennium and the bridge to the third. It is not a new message but can be considered a gift of special enlightenment that helps us to relive the Gospel of Easter more intensely, to offer it as a ray of light to the men and women of our time. What will the years ahead bring us? What will man's future on earth be like? We are not given to know. However, it is certain that in addition to new progress there will unfortunately be no lack of painful experiences. But the light of divine mercy, which the Lord in a way wished to return to the world through Sr. Faustina's charism, will illuminate the way for the men and women of the third millennium."

The Pontiff also stressed the need to pay attention to these messages.

"It is important then that we accept the whole message that comes to us from the word of God on this Second Sunday of Easter, which from now on throughout the Church will be called *"Divine Mercy Sunday."* In the various readings, the liturgy seems to indicate the path of mercy, which while re-establishing the relationship of each person with God, also creates new relations of fraternal solidarity among human beings. Christ has taught us "man not only receives and experiences the mercy of God, but is also called" to practice mercy towards others: "Blessed are the merciful, for they shall obtain mercy" (Mt 5: 7) (*Dives en Misericordia*, n. 14). He also showed us the many paths of mercy, which not only forgives sins but also reaches out to all human needs. Jesus bent over every kind of human poverty, material and spiritual. His message of mercy continues to reach us through His hands held out to suffering man. This is how Sr. Faustina saw Him and proclaimed Him to people on all the continents when, hidden in her convent at Lagiewniki in Krakow, she made her life a hymn to mercy: Misericordias Domini in aeternum cantabo."

Then in summation the Pope stressed how the message and *The Image* should be made known to all mankind:

"Sr. Faustina's canonization has a particular eloquence: by this act I intend today to pass this message on to the new millennium. I pass it on to all people, so that they will learn to know ever better the true face of God and the true face of their brethren."

Among the participants in the ceremonies were the president of the Polish government's Council of Ministers, and the president of Solidarity. In his remarks to the Polish pilgrims, the Pope noted, "This is a very special day for our country."

Pope John Paul II himself was clearly delighted and as he made the announcement proclaiming Faustina the first Saint of this Century thunderous applause could be heard throughout the streets of Rome. In what was clearly a moment of great pride for the many pilgrims from Poland many of whom were carrying their Polish flags as they personally witnessed their nation's favorite son proclaim their favorite daughter a Saint. It was an historical moment in the history of their country as they heard the Pope proclaim that henceforward, the first Sunday after Easter would be known throughout the Church as *Divine Mercy Sunday*. Five years later on this very same day even bigger crowd would ascend on Saint Peter's to mark the first day of Pope John Paul II's ascent towards his heavenly reward.

Chapter Fourteen

Papal seal of approval

What was it about Faustina's messages of mercy that prompted Pope John Paul II to catapult her to Sainthood? After all, the concept of God's Divine mercy is not new in either the Christian or the Jewish faiths and certainly was not exclusive to *The Diary of Saint Faustina*. In fact, throughout the history of the Church there are countless references to the Mercy of God which might explain why many within the Church do not find anything particularly unique about Faustina's revelations, and still till this day, can not fully comprehend the late Pontiff's devotion to her. Yet while the overriding theme of *The Diary* is not original, it is way beyond being just a reminder of God's mercy and this might explain why Faustina was canonized so quickly.

Indeed, there are many references to the mercy of God that can be found throughout scripture and in the testimonies of various Saints. The Holy Bible has no less than over 400 direct references to the mercy of God and there are numerous indirect references as well. Fifty-five of the Psalms for example, praise God's mercy and belief in a merciful God, and this is one of the chief characteristics of the Jewish faith. In fact the entire Holy Bible in many ways is a record of God's mercy toward mankind. Thus, given the fact that mercy is such a recurring theme throughout the history of the Jewish and Christian faiths, what was it about this diary of

Faustina's and her particular devotion to *The Divine Mercy* that prompted a Papal seal of approval so quickly? To answer this question, perhaps another question could be asked: Within all of the aforementioned testimonies and texts, has there ever been another message from Christ with such a strong emphasis on *His Divine Mercy*, the purpose of which was to specifically prepare the world for His return? Another important question of course would be the following: Have any other messages throughout the history of the Church ever been accompanied by a divinely inspired and commissioned Image? This pattern is entirely unique and despite the numerous messages of mercy which have been imparted to other Saints throughout history, in no other prophetic message has this very unique and solemn combination been brought together—not even in the Bible itself.

For while the Bible is indeed full of stories of mercy and teaches us "to be merciful as [our] Father in Heaven is merciful" (Luke: 6:36) and while it reveals the ultimate act of God's Mercy through the Passion and death Jesus endured to pay our debt for sin—and though in the New Testament there are numerous references to God's mercy, there yet remains no other individual apart from Faustina who was specifically told. *"I am sending you with My mercy to the people of the whole world."* (Diary entry 1588) This may be one of the reasons that prompted Faustina to write: **"There is one mystery, which unites me with the Lord of which no one – not even angels may know." (Diary entry 824)**

Indeed it is important to bear in mind the manner in which some other Saints referred to God's mercy in order to understand what separated Faustina from every one else.

It was in the year 373, St. Athanasius wrote, "It is the great Mercy of God that He becomes the Father of those to whom He is first the Creator." A few years later in 397, St. Ambrose stated, "Mercy, also, is a good thing, for it makes men perfect, in that it imitates the perfect Father. Nothing graces the Christian soul so much as mercy." In the next century around 407, St. John Chrysostom would explain, "Everything that God does is born of His Mercy and His clemency." Twenty-seven years later, St. Augustine prayed, "I confess, O Lord, that Thou art merciful in all Thine acts." Elsewhere he explained that "God's Mercy is not lacking to any of His works," and "Man, created in the image of God, is not of the same nature as God, and therefore is not His true son, but he becomes

His son through the grace of Divine Mercy." A century later St. Benedict taught that one should "never despair of God's mercy." Then seven hundred years later in 1274, St. Thomas Aquinas expressed his firm belief that, "God's mercy is the chief motive of all His external activity."

In a fascinating confirmation of Faustina's revelations, St. Gertrude the Great (d.1302) was reportedly given an identical Chaplet to the Mercy of God as imparted to Sister Faustina. The distinction of course, is that St. Gertrude was not commissioned to prepare the world for the very return of Christ. Even the great Doctor of the Church, St. Catherine of Siena (d.1380) once passionately prayed, "*Oh, Divine Mercy!*"

In an interesting twist to this story, it was just a few years before Faustina began receiving her instructions, that Sister Benigna Consolata, an Italian Visitation Nun was apparently told to say in her heart words similar to those later given to Saint Faustina "I have a Jesus, and I trust in Him," Yet this message was not followed by any great instructions to prepare the whole world for the coming of Christ. Indeed while many of these messages reiterate the theme of *Faustina's Diary*, clearly her mission was a very specific and global one. In addition, as we have already discussed, it would be a Polish Pope,—perhaps the most renowned Pope in history that would eventually and very enthusiastically carry the baton of this global mission.

In order to fully understand the importance that Pope John Paul II placed on Faustina's messages, let us look at what the late Holy Father said two years after Faustina's canonization while presiding over a ceremony in Poland in 2002. It was there in front of a capacity crowd in Krakow on August 18, when John Paul II entrusted the world to *The Divine Mercy* and dedicated the new shrine adjacent to Faustina's former convent in Lagiewniki. The Pope explained that this pilgrimage center, built over three years near the convent where Faustina Kowalska had lived and died, will spread the message of this Polish mystic "to all the inhabitants of the earth." Clearly John Paul saw this message as one of international significance! In fact the dedication of *the Divine Mercy Shrine* was the most important event of the 98th international trip of his pontificate, a fact which the decoration and preparation of this event attested to. The white surfaces on both sides of the altar projected video pictures that allowed 4,000 people present to see the figure of the Pope close-up. It was indeed a major event for the people of Poland. Having seen Faustina canonized and now this shrine erected, they knew that just as Pope John Paul II had done through his distinguished papacy, Faustina too would continue to bring honor to their country. John Paul also saw this as yet another opportunity to show the world the Image and consequently, above an enormous golden tabernacle shaped like the globe is a copy of the Image of the Merciful Jesus which had been imparted to Faustina. It is surrounded by a bush shaken by the wind, an Image of the struggle of humanity against our collective and personal weaknesses.

In fact, Pope John Paul II said during his homily:

"In this shrine, I wish solemnly to entrust the world to Divine Mercy. I do so with the burning desire that the message of God's merciful love, proclaimed here through St. Faustina, may be made known to all the peoples of the earth and fill their hearts with hope."

It is not hard to imagine what the Pope would think of the world today when back in 2002 he was already deeply concerned for the future of humanity: "How greatly today's world needs God's mercy! In every continent, from the depth of human suffering, a cry of mercy seems to rise up," the Holy Father exclaimed.

"Where hatred and the thirst for revenge dominate, where war brings suffering and death to the innocent, there the grace of mercy is needed in order to settle human minds and hearts and to bring about peace... Wherever respect for life and human dignity are lacking, there is need of God's merciful love, in whose light we see the inexpressible value of every human being... Mercy is needed in order to ensure that every injustice in the world will come to an end in the splendor of truth... From here, there must go forth 'the spark which will prepare the world for his final coming'... This spark needs to be lighted by the grace of God... This fire of mercy needs to be passed on to the world. In the mercy of God the world will find peace and mankind will find happiness!"

The heat of the day and of the crowded shrine affected the Pope, but he did not shorten the long rite of consecration of the church. At one point, clearly carried away by emotion, John Paul II said spontaneously: "Who would have thought that someone who walked here with wooden clogs would one day consecrate this basilica?" The Pope was referring to the fact that, just a few meters from the shrine is the site of the Solvay quarry where he worked in his youth during the Nazi occupation.

At the end of the ceremony, John Paul II met with Poland's former President Lech Walesa, who had previously led the Solidarity labor union. Things had certainly changed for Poland and the world since the days when these men were young. Yet, in their own way, they each had contributed greatly in their own ways toward the transformation of Poland. Now just as the Solidarity movement had transformed his former homeland, the Pope believed that Faustina's messages from Christ could transform the world. He had always known there was much to her Diary and rereading it during his rehabilitation, following the attempt on his life; he had become more convinced that the messages must be shared with all mankind.

About 20,000 people followed the ceremony outside the shrine and the crowds spilled over into the streets where the sound from the loud-speakers could scarcely be heard. Despite the distance, adults and young people remained kneeling in silence on the tarmac and pavements as if they were close to the altar. Following the ceremony, more than 200,000 people waited to catch a glimpse of the Holy Father as he passed by in the pope mobile.

The pope's desire to let the whole world see the Image and learn of the messages was heightened by events following St Faustina's canonization. John Paul was well aware of the various problems facing humanity since the turn of this century and as the Vicar of Christ, he was able to perceive these things not only through his natural intelligence, but also through his extraordinary spiritual discernment and many believe mystical ability.

Furthermore since proclaiming Faustina a Saint in 2000, the Pope was well aware of the direction the world was heading. He had witnessed the destruction of the Twin Towers in America and it pained him deeply. Indeed, this was a topic he addressed in his message for the World day of Peace on January 1, 2002.

Recent events, including the terrible killings {of September 11, 2001}, moves me to return to a theme that often stirs in the depths of my heart when I remember the events of history that have marked my life, especially my youth. The enormous suffering of peoples and individuals, even among my own friends and acquaintances, caused by Nazi and Communist totalitarianism has never been far from my thoughts and prayers. I have often paused to reflect on the persistent question: How do we restore the moral and social order subjected to horrific violence? My reasoned conviction, confirmed in turn by biblical revelation, is that the shattered order cannot be fully restored except by a response that combines justice with forgiveness. The pillars of true peace are justice and the form of love that is forgiveness. However, in the present circumstances, how can we speak of justice and forgiveness as the source and condition of peace? We can and we must, no matter how difficult this may be, a difficulty that often comes from thinking that justice and forgiveness are irreconcilable. Nevertheless, forgiveness is the opposite of resentment and revenge, not of justice. In fact true peace is "the work of justice" (Isa. 32.17). As a second Vatican Council put it, peace is "the fruit of that right ordering of things with which the divine founder has invested human society and which must be actualized by man thirsting for an ever more perfect reign of justice.

Also haunting the Pope in the last years of his life was the onslaught of natural disasters. He was well aware and had seen first hand the changes in global weather patterns and watched in horror with the rest of us as the tsunami devastated much of Indonesia in December 2004. Additionally, he also saw what he believed was a moral decline transpiring throughout the world and this broke his heart. There was clearly one thing John Paul believed he had to do before he died and this was to bring the world's attention to the message of *Divine Mercy*, the same message that had so profoundly shaped the very basis of his legendary pontificate.

CHAPTER FIFTEEN

DEATH OF POPE JOHN PAUL II

It was one of those moments in time that most of us will never forget. Just a few days after Easter Sunday, 2005, and the time when the Catholic Church was celebrating the run up to Divine Mercy Sunday, the celebration re -installed in 2000 because of the messages in Faustina's Diary.

As the world watched, it seemed that the Pope was certainly nearing the end of his time here on earth. It was indeed, a sad finale to a heroic man who had been an inspiration to the entire human family.

Certainly throughout his distinguished Papacy John Paul had been a paternal figure to many people. This is fitting of course in light of the fact the word pope actually means father. In ancient Greek it was a child's term of affection for the father of the family, but was borrowed later by the Latin as an honorific title. Both Greek-speaking Eastern and Latin-speaking Western Catholics then applied it to Priests, Bishops, and Patriarchs as heads of their spiritual families. Today, priests of the Orthodox Churches of Greece, Russia, and Serbia still refer to their parish priests as pope. Gradually, however, Latin Christianity began to restrict its usage, and at the beginning of the 3rd century, papa was a term of respect for clergy in high positions. By the 5th century, it was applied particularly to the Bishop of Rome, without excluding other usages. After the 8th century, however, as far as the West was concerned, the title was exclusively used for the Bishop of Rome. The great reforming Pope, Gregory VII (1073-1085), officially restricted its use to the Bishop of Rome. When applied to Pope John Paul II, the title conjured up a very personal connection and for millions he was truly their spiritual Father.

News of the ailing Pontiff's final moments followed months of concern about his health. He was initially hospitalized at the Rome's Gemilli hospital in February with symptoms of flu. A global outpouring of prayers and messages of love and support followed, and on February 3, 2005, the Pontiff received a message from Mehmet Ali Agca, who in 1981 had tried to kill him. Issuing a statement via his lawyer, Agca extended his good wishes for a speedy recovery, and called for the Pope to acknowledge that the world has come close to an end. In the brief statement hand written in Italian and then faxed to news agencies by his lawyer, Mustafa Demirbag, Agca said:

> Dear Pope John Paul II, you and I suffer for the fulfillment of a divine universal plan... I thank you for having revealed on May 13, 2000, the third secret of Fatima... Dear Pope, you must now confirm that we are at the end of the world. This is the last generation of humanity on Planet Earth. Only like this will God give you health and miraculous strength for the coming years. In any case, I embrace you Karol Wojtyla. I give you my best wishes.

What this would be assassin meant by these words is unclear, however, we do know that by spring of 2005, Pope John Paul II was certainly enduring a physical roller coaster. The Pope had returned to the hospital in March and a series of infections and accompanying high fever only made matters worse. For Catholics, this was happening during Lent and it seemed that the Pope in his suffering and pain was truly walking the way of the Cross. Yet this man who had endured two gunshot wounds in 1981, had a pre cancerous tumor removed from his colon in 1994, and who had suffered from Parkinson's disease for years, battled on. Observers during his Easter Blessing however witnessed the Pope in great discomfort. In fact, at many times during his address he started shaking and occasionally put his hands to his head. He even struggled to pronounce the words, "In the name of the Father."

For the first time in his long Papacy the Pope would have to delegate Easter ceremonies to his Cardinal, a reality which brought great sadness to the millions of the faithful around the world who consider Easter one of the most important events in the religious calendar.

Following Easter Sunday, and as the week progressed, it was becoming increasingly evident that the Pope's condition had worsened. Pope John Paul II, was now gravely ill with heart and breathing problems and the world knew a love affair with a much beloved man was nearing its end. The White House issued a statement that President George. W. Bush and his wife Laura had joined those around the world praying for John Paul. Surprisingly, even China wished the Pope a speedy recovery, an action, which marked the communist state's first public message to a head of the Catholic Church since the 1950's. Beijing insists its Catholics only worship in state approved Churches. In fact many Chinese Catholics continue to risk arrest by honoring the Pope in clandestine ceremonies. Catholics in Asia and South America meanwhile flocked to churches for special prayer meetings. These scenes were repeated all over the world. In the Brazilian city of San Paulo, some 20,000 people gathered to pray "We know how much he loves Brazil and also how much we Brazilians love the Pope," the city's archbishop, Cardinal Claudio Hummes, told the congregation.

In unison and all over the world prayers could be heard. In Mexico thousands flocked to the holy city of Guadalupe to pray, as they did in the town of Bethlehem, the birthplace of Christ and in Sydney Australia, when Bishop Julian Porteous praised the Pope as "one of the great men of our time."

At around noon EST on April 2, 2005, Vatican officials announced that the Pope's condition had turned "very grave," his heart and kidneys were failing and his breathing was shallow. Despite his grave condition, Faustina the woman whose messages had helped shape his illustrious Papacy accompanied the Pontiff till the end. It was only moments after celebrating the vigil mass of Divine Mercy— re-instated because of what was contained in the Dairy—when the Pope's reign on earth would end.

It was 21:37 pm in Rome, and already Divine Mercy Sunday in many parts of the world, a moment in time when people across the globe joined forces in prayer.

However, this would not be the Pope's last connection to Divine Mercy. His homily for the following days of celebrations had already been prepared and as thousands gathered in St Peter's Square, the next morning, as the Vatican secretary of state, Cardinal Angelo Sodano, concluded the Mass for the repose of Pope John Paul II's soul, the thousands gathered were given a gift—the last words that John Paul ever wrote, written before he died and on the subject of Divine Mercy. It was an interesting sense of timing when Archbishop Leonardo Sandri, Substitute of the Secretariat of State, said, "I have been charged to read you the text that was prepared in accordance with his explicit instructions by the Holy Father John Paul II. I am deeply honored to do so, but also filled with nostalgia." Included in the Pope's final words were the following statements;

> "As a gift to humanity, which sometimes seems bewildered and overwhelmed by the power of evil, selfishness, and fear, the Risen Lord offers his love that pardons, reconciles, and reopens hearts to love. It is a love that converts hearts and gives peace. How much the world needs to understand and accept Divine Mercy! Lord, who reveals the Father's love by your death and Resurrection; we believe in you and confidently repeat to you today: Jesus, I trust in you, have mercy upon us and upon the whole world."

There is an ironic sweetness in the fact that this famous and revered holy man who had written thousands of homilies, numerous encyclicals and countless words, would conclude his Papacy with words once imparted to the poor humble Polish woman who Jesus Christ called his "secretary."

PART THREE:

THE TRUE FACE OF CHRIST

Having examined Faustina's journey in both life and death, we will now examine what Christ was telling her and what it may possibly mean. Why was Faustina catapulted to Sainthood? Why were these messages so important for Pope John Paul II? Why were the last words the Pope left us, the very words found on The Image? As we will see, it is in Turin, Italy that the pieces of this mystical puzzle begin to take shape.

Chapter Sixteen

The Image and the Shroud.

Joseph bought a linen sheet, took the body down, wrapped it in the sheet, and placed it in a tomb which had been dug out of solid rock .- Mark 15.46

In the Cathedral of Turin, jealously guarded there for over five centuries by the House of Savoy, is a venerated shroud whose fame has reached every part of the world, arousing the interest of historians, physicists, archeologists, and theologians. It is a burial sheet of fine linen; similar to others that have come down to us from the ancient world, but unique because of the presence of its extraordinary discolorations. On the shroud, in a color between carmine and mauve, there appears the faint image of a man who died after long and indescribable suffering.

If we study the body with great care, and we contemplate the incomparable face, if we compare the marks, the wounds and the signs of blows with the account contained in the Gospels, we are struck with amazement. Everything coincides. Thus we have very valid reasons to believe that this could indeed be the Holy Shroud, and on it, both suffering and glorious, the image of Jesus Christ. The Shroud is one of the incalculable number, of God's gifts, the kerygma (proclamation) of the salvation announced by the Church. It is:

The wonderful document of His Passion, Death, and Resurrection, written for us in letters of blood. **—Pope Paul VI**

Astonishingly, when Faustina's Image of Christ is superimposed onto the image of this Holy Shroud, it provides a perfect match. This of course begs the question: If the Shroud of Turin were truly the image of Christ, then would this not also validate the Image of Divine Mercy as authentic? Indeed, according to a thousand-year-old tradition, the Shroud is recognized as the burial sheet of Christ, and scientific breakthroughs towards the end of the twentieth Century have concurred that this is an admissible claim. Church history also provides us with ancient testimonies that bear witness to the presence and veneration of a "Sacred Shroud" or "Sacred Face" dating back to the first centuries of Christianity. In fact, documented history concerning the actual Shroud of Turin first appeared around 1352 when it first reached Lirey in France. In 1454 the Shroud became the property of Louis, Duke of Savoy who transferred it to Chambery. As of 1502 it has been kept in a silver box which is displayed in a niche in the choir-sacristy wall of the gothic Sainte Chapelle built especially for the Shroud. The church was called Sainte Chapelle because, like the older one in Paris, it was designed to house relics of Christ's passion. Tragically in 1532 at some point during the night of December 3-4, a fire broke out in the choir-sacristy of the Sainte Chapelle causing some damage to the Shroud. It was restored two years later by the Poor Clares of Chambery.

The Shroud would be taken to its present resting place on September 14, 1578, when Duke Emanuel Philibert transferred the Shroud to Turin.

The first exposition of the Holy Shroud in Turin was celebrated in 1898. It was the 50th anniversary of the Constitution granted by King Charles Albert in 1848 and the 400th anniversary of the building of the present Cathedral. Indeed, it was during the exposition, that the first photograph of the Shroud was taken by its owners, The House of Savoy. In what appears to have been a miraculous occurrence, the result was truly amazing. The photograph produced a negative image when a positive should have been achieved. As a result of the first photographs, scholars then asked for further photographs to be taken. The most impressive of these was the one which revealed the Holy Face of Jesus, and as a result speculation about the shroud's authenticity began. In 1980 when Pope John Paul II made an historic pilgrimage to the Shroud, speculation over its Divine significance increased. Three years later when King Umberto handed over the Shroud's ownership to the Vatican, further curiosity was aroused. Additionally, on his historic visit, Pope John Paul, began distributing pictures of the Holy Face to a group of young members of Catholic Action and said:

> These are not pictures of the Blessed Virgin, it is true, but pictures that remind us as no other can. Since they are pictures of her Divine Son, and so, we can truly say, the most moving, loveliest, dearest ones that we can imagine.

John Paul was not the only pope who held a special reverence for the shroud. During a broadcast in 1953, Pope Pius XII, a man admired for his deep spirituality, amazing culture, and acute intelligence, stated of the Holy Shroud that it: "displays to our compunction and consolation, the image of the lifeless body and exhausted Divine Face of Jesus."

Indeed, further acceptance of the Divine origin of this image was provided by the man nicknamed "Good Pope John," who proclaimed *Digitus Dei est hic!*" (The finger of God is in this). While, Pope John Paul II, who first visited the Shroud as a Cardinal and returned to venerate it as Pope, said of the sacred linen cloth:

"The image of human suffering is reflected in the Shroud. It reminds modern man, often distracted by prosperity and technological achievements, of the tragic situation of his many brothers and sisters and invites him to question himself about the mystery of suffering in order to explain its causes."

While one might be led to assume that it would only be natural for the Catholic Church to fully endorse the Shroud, and even if we put aside all the scientific studies validating its authenticity, let us consider just the study based on the balance of probabilities that was made by Professor Bruno Barberis of the University of Turin. As part of his study Barberis revived the previous investigations of Yves Delage, Paul De Gail, and Tino

Zeuli. His method of research, while of absolute scientific rigor, was based on very simple considerations. The premise of his study being this:

If you throw a coin up in the air, the odds are two to one (1/2) it will land on the side you have chosen.

1.   Both Jesus and the Man of the Shroud were wrapped in winding sheets after death by crucifixion. Note that not many crucified men had a regular burial. (It was the most ignominious of punishments, reserved for slaves, brigands and murderers. The contempt for the man was also often extended to the corpse as well): one chance in a hundred (1/100).

2.   Both Jesus and the Man of the Shroud had a cap of thorns put on his head. No historical document mentions any such usage. In fact, the only reason that a crown of thorns was placed on Jesus' head was because the Roman centurions were mocking Jesus' claim to be a king. Let us limit this very remote probability to one in five thousand (1/5000).

3.   The patibulum weighed heavily on the shoulders of The Man of The Shroud as also Jesus'. Only occasionally was the condemned man made to carry the horizontal beam of the cross to the place of execution: odds of two to one (1/2).

4.   Same odds (1/2) on the way the hands and feet were fixed to the wood of the cross. They could be fastened with nails but a simpler and quicker method was to tie them on with ropes.

5.   The Shroud displays a wound on the right side of the Man who was wrapped in it. John's Gospel (19:33-34) tells how in Jesus' case, "instead of breaking his legs, one of the soldiers pierced his side with a lance, and immediately out came blood and water." Odds perhaps of one to ten (1/10).

6.   The Man of the Shroud had been wrapped in the sheet as soon as he was lowered from the cross: no washing or anointing of the corpse took place. It was the same with Jesus, since Jewish Passover was about to begin, during which no manual labor could be performed: odds of twenty to one (1/20.)

7.   The Shroud bears the imprint of a man's corpse, but no traces of putrefaction. Hence it wrapped a human body for a brief period though long enough for an imprint to be formed on it. In addition, did not the corpse of Jesus rest in the tomb for little more than thirty hours, from Friday evening until dawn on Sunday? This is an extraordinary case of agreement, which we may rate at odds of five hundred to one (1/500).

From this analysis, Barberis then obtained the aggregate probability: this given by the aggregate total of the individual probabilities considered, viz:

1/100 x 1/500 x 1/ 2 x 1 / 10 x 1 /20 x 1/500 = 1/200.000.000.000

In line with the scholars who preceded him, his findings concluded that out of 200 billion victims of crucifixion, only one could have possessed the same identical characteristics common to Jesus, the Man of the Shroud. The Gospel tells us his name is Jesus Christ, who suffered died, and was buried and who on the third day rose again from the dead.

Now consider the chances of a poor Polish Catholic nun, who knew nothing of the Shroud of Turin claiming to receive a vision of Christ in which he instructs her to have an image painted and that Image once finished ends up diametrically matching the Image on the Shroud precisely in every way. What would the odds be of this?

Yet, while the Shroud's authenticity continued to be the subject of debate, in January 2005 the findings of a report were released and seem to put to rest the authenticity of this sacred linen cloth once and for all. The new study based on new analysis of the shroud, suggests it is indeed between 1,300 and 3,000 years old. For though once dismissed as a medieval fake after scientific studies in 1988, the new study reported it could actually date back to 1000BC.

For while the 1988 analysis used radiocarbon dating techniques and concluded it was a medieval fake, this more recent study, published in the US peer-review journal Thermochimica Acta, refutes the earlier findings and claims the sample used in the earlier research was taken from "an expertly rewoven patch" used to repair fire damage and, as such, does not give a true measure of its age.

Raymond Rogers, a chemist at the Los Alamos Laboratory in New Mexico, who conducted the tests, said: "As unlikely as it seems, the sample used to test the age of the Shroud of Turin in 1988 was taken from a rewoven area.

He went on: "The 1988 sample tested was dyed in Italy at about the time the Crusaders' last bastion fell to the Mameluke Turks in AD 1291. The radiocarbon sample cannot be older than about AD 1290, agreeing with the age determined in 1988. However, the shroud itself is actually much older."

Roger's statements are backed up by the fact that since its existence was first recorded, the shroud has been damaged in several fires, including a church inferno in 1532. As a result new patches were added which had been restored by nuns, who patched the holes and stitched the garment to a reinforcing material known as the Holland cloth.

The 1988 study, co-ordinated by the British Museum, which acted as the official clearing house for all its findings, apparently ruled out the possibility that the shroud wrapped the body of Christ but never took into account that it was restored because of fire damage, which led to the then Cardinal of Turin, Anastasio Alberto Ballestrero, saying the shroud was a hoax.

Since then, several attempts have been made to challenge the authenticity of that analysis and perhaps the greatest corroboration of the new study will be if the shroud's custodians permit further samples of the original, un-repaired cloth to be taken for radiocarbon analysis. We now know however, as a result of this more recent study that the shroud is old enough to be the actual cloth thus eliminating the one last remaining obstacle as to ascertaining its authenticity. All of these factors may help us to understand Pope John Paul's fascination with the shroud, and also why its ownership was handed over to the Vatican.

While the Shroud functions as a tool to remind us of the pain and suffering of Jesus' Passion, it also stands as a witness to the historical reality of Christ's death, burial, and resurrection. The Image of Divine Mercy is also a tool to remind us of the infinite mercy, and love of God for all people, and a witness to Christ's commission to Faustina to "Prepare the World for my final coming."

We shall now examine another twentieth Century discovery which seems to point towards a Divine plan for this moment in history.

Chapter Seventeen

Heaven Sent?

While the shroud of Turin is similar to others that have been handed down from the ancient world it is not the last piece of Divine evidence mankind has discovered in modern times. In fact less than ten years following Faustina's death, and a few years after the commissioning of her Divinely inspired image, a large collection of ancient biblical texts was discovered in the Holy Land. If we are among those who believe Rabbi Hecht's concept that, "God didn't create the universe and then step back to let it run by itself, but that He remains actively involved, pulling levers, pushing buttons and flipping switches behind the scenes" then this discovery of the Dead Sea Scrolls found mid-way through the 20th Century, would certainly be viewed as somewhat prophetic.

In what sounds rather like a biblical scenario, it was while three Bedouin shepherds, Khalil Musa, Jum'a Muhammad Khalil, and their younger cousin, Muhammad Ahmed el-Hamed were moving herds between Bethlehem and the River Jordan, they made this amazing discovery. During part of their daily routine these men would often discuss various prophets from the region and at times do a little exploring, attempting to rediscover the places where these people once lived. As the story is recounted, it was on a winter evening in or around 1947, when, Jum'a discovered two small openings in the side of a rock face near the ancient ruins of a place called

Qumran. He then threw a rock into the smaller of the two holes and, surprisingly, heard what sounded like the dull crack of breaking pottery. Jum'a called the other two over to the holes and told them what he had heard but because night was falling they decided to go home.

Two days later, eager to discover what hidden treasure might be inside the cave, the youngest shepherd, Muhammad Ahmed, returned. After squeezing through the larger hole to enter the cave, according to American scholar John Trever, author of *The Untold Story of Qumran,* "his eyes became accustomed to the dim light, and he saw about 10 tall jars lining the wall of the cave."

When Muhammad told the others of his discovery, they became angry that he had gone to the cave without them and so they all returned to the cave and Muhammad squeezed in again to recover anything they judged worth carrying. Eventually they came away with two bundles wrapped in cloth, covering two parchment scrolls, and one leather scroll without a cover. At the time they had no way of knowing that what they had discovered were the Ancient and Sacred documents, which would come to be known as The Dead Sea Scrolls—texts which perhaps more than any previous find, have reaffirmed the textual integrity of the Old Testament. Included in their findings was the entire book of Isaiah along with text from all but one other book, Esther, in the Hebrew Bible, which largely—if not precisely—confirmed the accuracy of later translations of the Bible. Following the initial discovery, The Dead Sea Scrolls eventually comprised 825-872 documents found between the first discoveries in 1947 and continuing through till 1956. All in all, the documents were discovered in eleven caves in and around the Wadi Qumran near the ruins of the ancient settlement of Khirbet Qumran, on the northwest shore of the Dead Sea. The texts are of great religious and historical significance, as they are practically the only known surviving biblical documents written before AD 100.

It is interesting that the community at Qumran historically had viewed themselves as living in the end-times. And with the scroll of Isaiah discovered in this region centuries later, a scroll pointing to a "messianic apocalypse" could be more than mere coincidence? According to James Vanderkam and Peter Flint, authors of *The Meaning of the Dead Sea Scrolls,* "The Qumranites believed they could read off coming events from prophecies, since God had already decreed what was going to happen."

The apocalypses found among the scrolls were discovered in cave eleven and have been referred to as *The War Rule*. Within this rule the text describes the eschatological (end-time) war in which the sons of light, who belong on the side of God, are opposed to the sons of darkness, whose leader is Belial. Vanderkam and Flint say that the particular focus of the War Rule is on the final series of seven battles between the forces of God and Satan, which will last forty years. In the first three battles, the Sons of Light will prevail, and in the next three the Sons of Darkness will have the advantage. With the two armies tied, in the seventh and final battle, the hand of God will prevail and the sons of darkness will be completely destroyed. Certainly, some themes in this description are echoed in the book of Revelation. Many believe the scrolls also provide a window into a formative period of both Judaism and Christianity, "a time for which we had virtually no first-hand knowledge prior to the discovery," according to scrolls scholar Martin Abegg Jr. of Trinity Western University in Langley, British Columbia. Nevertheless, do they also tell us something about our future?

Perhaps what surprised most people about the discovery of the scrolls was the fact nobody had been looking for them. Many have seen the combination of the confirming nature of the finds for the Hebrew Bible as well as the timing—namely at a time just prior to the re-establishment of the State of Israel—as pointing to the find as having been divinely guided. Were the Scrolls found just as Israel was being reinstated to remind the world of Israel's historical significance and of the place where Judaism and Christianity began? Why was the book of Isaiah, often referred to as the "Fifth Gospel," the only book discovered virtually intact? This is especially interesting considering who Isaiah was and what he had to say. Here was a man who from both a religious and political standpoint was witness to one of the most turbulent periods in the history of Jerusalem. Moreover, while Isaiah took an active and in some cases central role in the course of events, above all he was a man who put his faith in divine salvation. Could it also be that in allowing the discovery of these scrolls when the State of Israel was coming into creation that God wanted to remind us of what was said in Isaiah; that God will never forget the children of Israel?

Consider the fact that the timing of the scrolls also coincided with a time in history when new technologies would provide scholars with the ability to properly analyze and examine the texts. Beyond this, newer scientific breakthroughs have also enabled us to examine the DNA and microscopic evidences found within the Shroud of Turin, which some believe provide living proof of the physical divinity of Christ through His life, death, and resurrection. Which begs the question as to whether the Scrolls in turn act as a vehicle which enable us to re-confirm the existence of those living witnesses of God, prophets like Isaiah who were sent to warn us about the future? Does this correlate in any way to the message that Christ gave Faustina when He said, *In the Old Covenant, I sent prophets, wielding thunderbolts to My people. Today I am sending you with My mercy to the people of the world.* For if within the last fifty years we have been given reconfirmation of the prophets of old, are we likewise called to receive a modern day prophet—a woman who Pope John Paul II described as "The great Apostle of our times"?

Chapter Eighteen

Faustina's Image of Christ and Its Significance Today

As we have seen, it was only after a long series of delays that the Church officially approved Faustina's revelations. It would be several decades before the fulfillment of Christ's instructions to Faustina to make His messages known to the World. Yet could this timing all have had a very specific purpose in the Divine Plan? Were these messages only able to be fully understood at this moment in time when the world is in conflict over God?

When we consider all of the mysterious elements and the extraordinary developments in this story, we are left with many questions. It would take a seventy year journey and an extensive calling into question the credibility of the woman who Christ Himself called *"My Secretary"* before she would finally receive a Papal endorsement. Of course, this was only following the most thorough scrutiny; a complete investigation by the Catholic Church into Faustina's mental and psychological status, a thorough investigation into *the Diary's* authenticity, a Vatican ban on *the Diary* and *the Image*, and ultimately what could only be described as Divine intervention through Pope John Paul II. However, if one is truly convinced that Faustina's revelations are indeed revelations from God, then one must also recognize that in God's Providence, these delays must have had a purpose. In light of the timing of the delays, one can only conclude that the Divine purpose was that these messages would only be revealed when they could be better interpreted. Is it at all surprising then, that Faustina's official Church recognition would come only shortly before the onset of what is being viewed by much of the world as a global religious war?

Now, it is important to stress here that no matter what any individual might believe regarding religious matters, the overriding theme of these messages is that Christ loves everyone irrespective of whether they believe in him or not. So whether you accept or reject Jesus as Divine or even if you accept Christ as nothing more than an historical figure or prophet, it is of significant fascination that the messages imparted to this humble nun were intended to be shared with every one of us. However, it is also important to note that this study of Faustina's life and the interpretation of her role in Christ's plan are seen through her own Christian perspective. After all, Faustina's identity as a Catholic nun formed both her identity and her mission. To this end many of her messages and indeed the very *Image* itself may by definition contradict the tenets of other belief systems. Of course in such a politically correct and politically charged age, it becomes difficult to simply express one's beliefs without offending the sensibilities of someone from another belief system. That is most certainly not the intention here. What is submitted here however is the interpretation that Faustina would most identify with; it is offered within the context of the Christian belief that, according to the earliest historical Christian Creed, Jesus is both Lord and Savior and that "He will come again to judge the living and the dead." The purpose here is in no way to create any form of religious polemic, but rather to simply tell how the journey of one simple Catholic nun and her message seems to speak to what is happening in our much troubled world today. We leave you the reader, free to reach your own conclusions concerning this matter.

When considering all of the facts, we must note that the shared belief of the World's three most predominant religions regarding the anticipation of the Messiah's return come into conflict when one analyzes precisely whom it is that each faith awaits. In Judaism, they look forward to the Messiah—Christians await the return of Jesus Christ—and Muslims anticipate the coming of a man who will claim to be the Muslim Christ, known as *Isa Al-Maseeh*. The fundamental difference between the Muslim Jesus and his Christian counterpart is the fact that Islam states that he will deny that he is the Son of God and claim to be a Muslim. Historically of course these anticipations have always existed, but until this moment in time, they largely did not seem to matter. The world today however is in grave danger with a global jihad that at times seems as though it may threaten the very future of the free world.

In his book *Crossing the Threshold of Hope* John Paul II reached out to Muslims, praising them for the similarities that exist between Christianity and Islam:

The Church has the highest regard for Muslims, who worship one God, living and subsistant, merciful and omnipotent, the creator of heaven and earth. As a result of their monotheism, believers in Allah are particularly close to us.

The Pope however also pointed to some fundamental differences between the two religions:

Christ is unique! Unlike Muhammed, He does more than just promulgate principles of religious discipline to which all God's worshippers must conform... [Islam also presents us with] a God who is only Majesty, never Emmanuel, God - with – us. Islam is not a religion of redemption. There is no room for the cross and the Resurrection. Jesus is mentioned, but only as a prophet who prepares for the last prophet Muhammed. There is also mention of Mary, His Virgin Mother, but the tragedy of redemption is completely absent. For this reason not only the theology but also the anthropology of Islam is very distant from Christianity.

Nonetheless the Pope reminds us of the admirable qualities of discipline that exist within the lives of most Muslims.

The religiosity of Muslims deserves respect. It is impossible not to admire, for example, their fidelity to prayer. The image of believers in Allah who, without caring about time or place, fall to their knees in prayer remains a model for those who invoke the true God, in particular Christians while, having deserted their magnificent Cathedrals, pray only a little or not at all.

In keeping with the Pope's respect for those of the Muslim faith in the telling of this story, our perspective is from Faustina's viewpoint in that she was to help prepare the World for the return of Jesus Christ as the only Son of God.

To execute her mission, according to the words of Christ, an image would play a mysterious yet vital role. To unravel this part of the mystery, we need to begin with Christ's first message to His Secretary on February 22, 1931, where He stated:

> **Paint an image according to the pattern, you see, with the Signature: Jesus, I trust in you. I desire that this Image be venerated, first in your chapel, and {then} throughout the whole world.**

> —Diary entry 47

When Sister Faustina first received the instructions from Christ to have an image painted, to prepare the world for his final coming, there was certainly no way for this young woman who had never left Poland to understand how this Image might be a matter of significance for the 21st Century and specifically for the *last-days*. In fact, one of the biggest difficulties in interpreting Faustina's revelations is in making a clear and understandable connection between Christ's call to *"prepare the world for my return,"* and *the Image of Divine Mercy.* On the surface, it certainly seems peculiar. One must wrestle to understand how a mere painting of Christ could help prepare the world for His return. However, perhaps in keeping with the consistent patterns of Divine revelation, the connection between Faustina's Image and the last-days—or Christ's return—was intended to be a mystery until the proper time. Perhaps it would require various world events to unfold before the mystery of Faustina's revelations could be illuminated and understood more fully.

Whichever way we choose to look at our world the facts are most evident and we are now witnessing uncertain times—a juncture in history when many are beginning to question what the future of the World might hold. Though for some it seemed that this simple nun's messages were intended to provide her native Poland with hope as they moved towards World War II, the mere fact that she was not known or canonized until decades later, it would seem that these messages were meant to be shared now, following her recognition as a Saint, and only after her reputation had received the endorsement of the most beloved Pope perhaps who has ever lived. There is indeed concrete evidence to suggest why the Messages and Image of Saint Faustina are intended for our current times.

In the nearly 70 years that it took for Faustina to be canonized, there is so much that has taken place. The world has witnessed the advancement of time and technology that would eventually come to dominate our lives. In over seven decades we have witnessed a tremendous global change in virtually every area of the world. Additionally, periods of instability have confronted almost every nation on our planet. When pondering the changes that have taken place in the World since Faustina's day there are certainly many things to consider. We have seen the reconstruction after World War II, the birth of the nation of Israel, the fall of the Soviet Union, and an utter explosion in technology and global communication. In fact there are it seems, no shortages of events and changes that have transformed the world since the 1930's. However, when we zoom in specifically to the year that Faustina was canonized, there is one issue that seems to stand out above all the others.

The global landscape and way of life has most certainly been horribly interrupted since September 11th 2001, the anniversary of the same date in 1683 when Christianity defeated Islam in Europe.

What began as a bright Tuesday morning centuries later was soon horribly darkened, as smoke and debris filled the air of the New York City skies. The winds of change came suddenly and quickly they seemed to spread the darkness of that day throughout the world.

Moreover, while at times we may forget, imagining that the world has returned to normal, the reality is that there now exists a threat to our way of life that is always hovering in the background. The feelings of unease are exacerbated by daily reports of new threats and new attacks. The constant banter of Iranian nuclear ambitions seems only to be the latest addition to the mixture of frightening daily news. We now seem to have almost become numb to the fact that since 9-11, 2001 fundamentalist Islam has become the dominating source of newspaper headlines. It seems the entire world is involved in the War on Terror and tragically this is not a war that will be over anytime soon. Though very few are using the term, many astute commentators have said that we are indeed in the early stages of World War III.

This all seems a far cry from the relative peace and prosperity of the last decades of the 20th Century—when a religious war certainly did not dominate the headlines. Indeed, few worried about the world being torn apart by religious hatred and violence, and if we think back to just before

9-11, before the turn of this century, the world was a very different place. International terrorism was something that happened far from America and did not exactly pose a major threat to our way of life. Now of course all this has changed. We now live in a world where there are terrorist sleeper cells in America, the Caribbean, across Europe and even China, who now threaten our world. It is a problem we now confront on a global scale which was certainly not a issue during Sister Faustina's lifetime.

During the 1930's, when Faustina received her revelations, much of the Muslim world was essentially a colonized and defeated entity. Many observers in fact explain Middle East anger towards the West today in terms of historical invasions and Western interference in that much-troubled region. Yet, in spite of this, what is being fought out is really a desire for Islamic domination of the whole world. Certainly no one could ever justify however the barbaric acts of terrorism which we have witnessed since the start of the 21st Century in the name of religion!

During Faustina's time however, the threatening element of Islam lay dormant. There was good reason for this. The Ottoman Empire had fallen and the Caliphate, the Islamic equivalent of The Papacy, had been abolished. The outlook for the future of the Muslim world was bleak. However, that has now all changed entirely. Since Faustina's day, we have seen, among other things, the establishment of the state of Israel and the resulting sense of unity among Muslims in their emotionally charged opposition to the Jewish nation. We have seen the birth and the growth of the Islamic Brotherhood in Egypt that has spawned literally dozens of other radical and terrorist networks worldwide. We have watched the influence of the Iranian Revolution spread throughout Lebanon and Syria through Hezbollah—*the party of Allah.* We have seen the powerful revival and growth of Wahabiism in Saudi Arabia and the Gulf nations. We have seen the defeat of the Soviet Union in Afghanistan and the establishment of the Taliban in that same country. We have seen the Muslim immigrant population in Europe explode. With the advent of the Internet and the easy communication and exchange of ideas, we have seen these radical groups throughout the world network in ways that would never have been possible before.

Islam has now gradually emerged as the premiere issue and challenge that much of the world is wrestling with and while a majority of Muslims seek a peaceful co-existence with non-Muslims, fundamentalist Islam is at war with its neighbors, its host nations, or even its own people in numerous nations. From Chechnya to Nigeria, from Kashmir to France, from Iraq to Sudan, from the Philippines to the Ivory Coast, radical Islam is fighting for supremacy. As Harvard Professor Samuel P. Huntington has commented, "Islam's borders are bloody, and so are its innards"

Shortly after the advent of Islam, there were two great forward surges of conquest and growth. The result was that the realm of Islam, as if suddenly, extended from Spain to Indonesia. Many astute observers and radical Muslims alike have declared that the third great Jihad is now commencing. Islam's goals of complete world domination are now within range, and many believe the blueprint for global Islamization is being tried out in Iraq and Gaza. Indeed, despite growing concerns about Allied forces in Iraq, Alimza Jafarzaden, author of Iran Threat, believes a much bigger issue is at stake. He says; "The main threat to Iraq is neither al Qaeda nor the Sunni insurgents – they both are cause for major problems, but neither can take the whole future of Iraq as hostage. Rather Iraq is now a battleground for the clash of two alternatives: the Islamic extremist option, which gets its orders form Tehran and seeks to establish an Islamic republic in Iraq, or a democratic alternative." The eventual outcome of this battle will no doubt shape the future of the Middle East and the world. The same can be said of Hamas in Gaza, where Israel now has a radical Islamist state as its neighbor. Either way Islam is no longer an issue that can be ignored. It has become the premiere challenge of the 21st Century. In truth, the world's richest religion is Islam, funded by both oil rich Saudi Arabia and Iran, Islam is able to export its fundamentalist interpretation of the Koran throughout the West. As a result Al Qaeda sympathizers can now literally be found in every country throughout the free world.

And so, it is not surprising then, that by taking a closer look at Islam, what many are now calling the religion of the future—its belief system, its own unique perspective on the end of the world, and most specifically its view of Jesus, we may actually find some of the most significant keys to unlock a deeper understanding of Faustina's revelations and why they were sent.

Nevertheless, beyond the curious timing issue—namely that within one year of Faustina's canonization, the issue of Islamic extremism was suddenly thrust onto the forefront of the World's attention—are there any other reasons to see a connection between Faustina's Messages, *The Image of Divine Mercy*, and the rise of Islamic extremism? In fact, there is a very significant "coincidence" that must also be briefly explored.

During the 8th and 9th centuries, a significant conflict broke out within the Christian Church. The conflict took place during a time when vast portions of the Byzantine Christian Empire were being influenced by its contact and conflict with the ever-expanding Islamic Empire. The conflict consisted of two factions; the first group was known as Iconodules and the second group was known as Iconoclasts. The Iconodules were those who supported the continued use of religious art, imagery, and iconography within the context of the Christian religious experience. The iconoclasts were those who caved into the pressure from the Muslim World, in which they were living or coming into increasing contact with. Orthodox Islam which forbids the use of all physical representations and religious imagery. The battle raged on for over five hundred years. During this time, the iconoclasts destroyed untold thousands of pieces of Christian liturgical art and icons. It was finally at the Second Council of Nicaea that the issue was completely settled. The Church decided in favor of the iconodules. The reasons were summarized in the notion that because God himself took on human flesh through the Incarnation of Christ—the perfect "Icon" of God— it was most certainly permissible to portray spiritual realities through material and physical media. Because Islam so fervently rejects the incarnation, it is only logical that they would also reject the use of religious imagery. Christianity however, as a uniquely and thoroughly *incarnational* religion, embraces the use of physical matter to facilitate worship of God.

Today the Eastern Orthodox Churches celebrate this triumph of incarnational theology as a feast once a year. "The Feast of The Triumph of Orthodoxy" or "The Sunday of Orthodoxy" has become one of the most celebrated feast days in the Eastern Calendar. On this day, the Eastern Churches carry out a triumphal procession of icons and also corporately declare an "Anathema" (curse) against all who claim that icons are not a part of the Christian liturgical experience. It is this Sunday that also begins Lent in preparation for Pascha—the name that the Eastern Church uses to refer to Easter. What is significant about this story with reference to *the Image of Divine Mercy* is that of all the days in the year, it was on this particular feast day, "the Sunday of Orthodoxy" that Christ spoke to

Saint Faustina, and commissioned her to have *the Image of Divine Mercy* painted.

The question must then be asked: Was Christ, in commissioning Faustina to paint an Image (literally "icon" in Greek) of Himself specifically on a day dedicated to the celebration of religious Images, mystically testifying against any such anti-incarnational theology, such as that which is embraced by Islam. More specifically was Christ testifying against the staunchly anti-incarnational Jesus of Islam? There are some strong reasons to suggest that this is precisely what Jesus was doing.

In order to contextualize these questions, we need to first understand some crucial warnings that Jesus Christ issued to his disciples shortly before his trial and crucifixion.

Most of us have heard the expression, "a wolf in sheep's clothing." Yet few may be aware that Jesus himself first coined this phrase. When Jesus first uttered this warning, he was speaking specifically about false prophets. The exact phrase was, "Watch out for false prophets. They come to you in sheep's clothing, but inwardly they are ferocious wolves" (Matthew 7:15). This theme is a common one in Jesus' sermons. Shortly before Jesus went to embrace the cross at Golgotha, his disciples asked him some very pertinent questions about His return and the last-days. As Jesus began to answer his disciples and explain the nature of the last-days, he warned against false prophets. "Watch out that no one deceives you. For many will come in my name, claiming, 'I am the Christ,' and will deceive many."

Jesus warned us all that the last-days would be terrible times when anti-Christian persecution and even execution would spread throughout the world, a sad reality which we are now facing. In fact, Jesus explained that many Christians would turn away from the faith—literally betraying one another to their persecutors and again, He warns of false prophets:

> *"Then you will be handed over to be persecuted and put to death, and you will be hated by all nations because of me. At that time many will turn away from the faith and will betray and hate each other, and many false prophets will appear and deceive many people. Because of the increase of wickedness, the love of most will grow cold, but he who stands firm to the end will be saved."*
>
> **—Matthew 24:9**

This portion of the Gospel of Matthew is replete with this type of warning, as if false prophets and false Christs were among Jesus's greatest concern.

"At that time if anyone says to you, 'look, here is the Christ!' or, 'There he is!' do not believe it. For false Christs and false prophets will appear and perform great signs and miracles to deceive even the elect—if that were possible. See, I have told you ahead of time. So if anyone tells you, 'There he is, out in the desert,' do not go out; or, 'Here he is, in the inner rooms,' do not believe it.
—Matthew 24:23

But then Jesus makes a statement that is rather difficult to understand initially. He says,

"For as lightning that comes from the east is visible even in the west, so will be the coming of the Son of Man. Wherever there is a carcass, there the vultures will gather."
—Matthew 24:28

Furthermore, according to Jesus' teachings, His return will be obvious, undeniable, and known to all the inhabitants of the earth. With this understanding, now we will contrast the biblical, historical Jesus of the Church—the Jesus of Faustina's revelations, with one anticipated by millions of people—namely radical Islam's expectation concerning Christ's return.

CHAPTER NINETEEN

THE JESUS OF CHRISTIANITY-THE JESUS OF ISLAM

In light of Jesus' many warnings that in the last-days, many false prophets would appear, even claiming to be the Christ, it is important that we understand who the Islamic Jesus is. For of all of the "other" supposed Jesuses that exist in the world, in light of the sheer exploding growth of Islam, it is the Islamic Jesus that is now the most looming "other Jesus" on earth, and one which Islam, as the world's fastest growing religion anticipates. Furthermore in light of various terror attacks on America and throughout the world Islamic extremists are affecting our lives with a view to eliminating Christianity, Judaism, along with every other belief or non belief system which doesn't conform to fundamentalist Islam. This trend is also affecting the lives of millions of peaceful Muslims as we witness atrocities usually confined to the streets of the Middle East and copycatted in the West and in other parts of the free world.

It is important then that we fully understand the global determination of radical Islam and examine the ancient texts of Islam, to fully comprehend what they are fighting for and who they believe the Islamic Jesus is. It is in the Islamic fundamentalist belief of Jesus where we are presented with a totally contradictory character to the historical and biblical Jesus of Faustina's revelations.

First, it must be understood Muslims reject the idea that Jesus was or is the Divine Son of God. According to the Qur'an, Islam's primary holy book, Jesus is not as the Bible articulates, the Word of God incarnate among us:

In blasphemy indeed are those that say that God is Christ the son of Mary.
—Surah 5:17

The Jews call 'Uzair a son of Allah and the Christians call Christ the son of Allah. That is a saying from their mouth; (in this) they but imitate what the unbelievers of old used to say. *Allah's curse be on them: how they are deluded away from the Truth!*
—Surah 9:30

The Quran literally pronounces a curse on those who believe that Jesus is God's Son. According to the Quran, those who believe such a thing believe a "monstrous falsehood" and are likened to "unbelievers" (i.e. infidels and idol worshippers).

Secondly, according to Islamic belief, Jesus never died on the cross for the sins of mankind.

Additionally, among Islamic scholars, there are actually numerous conflicting theories regarding exactly what happened to Jesus. Despite the inability to arrive at any consensus regarding what happened to Jesus, they are very much in agreement on at least one issue: *He was not crucified!* This passage of the Quran makes at least this much clear. In fact, according to Muslim scholars, Jesus never even experienced death. Instead, Muslims believe that when the authorities came to seize Jesus in order to crucify him, Allah miraculously delivered Jesus, after which he was assumed into heaven alive. Since then, Muslims believe, Jesus has remained with Allah in a sort of frozen state, awaiting his opportunity to return to the earth to finish his ministry and complete his life. As such, to the Islamic mind, Jesus was not in any way a "savior" who died for the sins of the world. In addition, while Muslims maintain the title "messiah" for Jesus, he has truly been stripped of any genuine messianic characteristics. Therefore, in general terms, Islam teaches that Jesus is merely another prophet in the long line of prophets that Allah has sent to mankind—although from the

Christian perspective there is at least one very important difference, Jesus is the Son of God.

In light of the fact that Faustina's legacy has left us with a divinely commissioned Image of Jesus and because her messages have such an eschatological emphasis, it therefore becomes important to understand the looming eschatological Jesus of Islam. Many people are surprised to learn that in Islam, as in Christianity, Jesus is also expected to return to the earth from heaven. Christians often get very excited by this fact as they see it as a possible bridge of agreement between the two religions. Unfortunately, the Islamic belief of who this Jesus is and what he does once he has arrived, is drastically different than what Christians believe.

In order to understand the Islamic concept of Jesus' return, the first thing that needs to be realized is that when Jesus comes back, *he comes back as a radical Muslim*! Muslims believe that Christianity and Judaism are merely distortions of the one true religion that was preached and practiced by the various "prophets" who were sent at various times in history. As such, Muslims believe that when Jesus was on the earth, he was a devout Muslim—preaching the message of Islam. Likewise, Muslims believe that when Jesus returns to the earth, he will continue this very same ministry. We will discuss exactly what it is that Muslims believe that Jesus will accomplish when he returns, but first, we need to take a small diversion to spotlight another very unusual and frightening man whose brief presence on the world political scene has made quite an impact.

The Islamic concept of Jesus is one upheld by the President of Iran as is evident when on September 17, 2005, Mahmoud Ahmadinejad addressed the United Nations National Assembly in New York City. American President George W. Bush sat in attendance. Concluding his speech, Ahmadinejad made a plea to Allah to speedily bring forth the emergence of Islam's mysterious Messiah figure known as Imam Al-Mahdi .

These are some very concerning facts about Ahmadinejad: He is largely rumored to be a member of a radical Islamic zealot group called Hojjatieh. Hojjatieh believe that it will only be after its adherents unleash utter chaos in the earth that the long-awaited Mahdi will emerge. What will ensue will be a triumphant period of Islamic style justice throughout the world. Additionally, Ahmadinejad has adamantly continued his pursuit of Iranian nuclear capabilities. The Iranian President has also, and repeatedly called for the destruction of America and Israel.

Furthermore, in what appeared to be a reflection of the methods used by many of the earliest Muslim Caliphs, during the early days of the Islamic conquests, Ahmadninejad even wrote a letter to President Bush calling on him to convert to Islam. Shockingly, Ahmadinejad has repeatedly claimed that the emergence of the Mahdi will take place within the next few years.

Unquestionably, Ahmadinejad is a man whom the world needs to keep their eyes on. He is a radical Muslim whose two primary emphases seem to be achieving Iranian nuclear capability and preparing for the soon emergence of the Islamic warlord known as the Mahdi. While it certainly seems unlikely that there will genuinely emerge a man who the Muslim world will acknowledge as Imam Al-Mahdi within just the next few years, it is certainly worth noting that the call for the emergence of the Mahdi has reached a place of prominence and urgency within fundamentalist Islam. This is the man, as we have pointed out; that the Muslim world believes will be followed by Jesus when he returns. According to Islamic tradition, upon Jesus' return, the Mahdi will be about to lead his Muslim army in prayer. The Mahdi will invite Jesus to lead them in prayer but Jesus will decline, and instead will pray behind the Mahdi as a direct sign of his deference to the Mahdi as the leader of all Muslims. Thus the Islamic Jesus is believed by most Muslims to become the Mahdi's second in command. Aware of this very frightening concept, let us now return to our discussion of the Islamic teachings regarding Jesus' final mission on the earth.

> *Beyond all of these traditions regarding Jesus, there are also Islamic beliefs that pertain specifically to the physical appearance of the Islamic Jesus. Their relevance to the study of Faustina and her revelations to the world are crucial. First however, let us look at the description of Jesus as penned by the pagan Priest of Judea, who in his official capacity sent a report to the Roman Senate under the Emperor Tiberius Caesar. This man was an eyewitness to Christ but certainly not a believer in his teachings. The following words were taken from the original manuscript:*

> *"There appeared in these our days, a man of great virtue, named Jesus Christ, who is yet living among us, and*

144

of the gentiles is accepted for a prophet of truth, but his own disciples call him the Son of God – he raiseth the dead and cureth all manner of diseases.

A man of stature somewhat tall and comely, with very reverend countenance, such as the beholders may both love and fear – his hair of the colour of chestnut full ripe, plain to the ears, whence downward, it is more orient and curling and wavering about the shoulders. In the midst of the head is a seam or partition in his hair, after the manner of the Nazarites. His forehead plain and very delicate, his face without spot or wrinkle beautified with a lovely red, his nose and mouth formed as nothing can be reprehended; his beard thick in colour like his hair- not very long, but forked: his look innocent and mature; his eyes grey, clear and quick. In reproving he is terrible; in admonishing courteous and fair spoken; pleasant in conversation, mixed with gravity. It can not be remembered that any have seen him laugh, but many have seen him weep. In proportion of body, most excellent; his hands and arms most delicate to behold. In speaking very temperate, modest and wise. A man, for his singular beauty, surpassing the children of men."

Now let us consider four traditional Islamic descriptions of Jesus' physical appearance.

The Prophet (May God bless him and grant him peace) said: "On the night of Isra' [his miraculous journey from Makkah to Jerusalem] I met Moses-he was a slim man with wavy hair, and looked like a man from the Shanu'ah tribe. I also met *Jesus-he was of medium height and of a red complexion,* as if he had just come out of the bath.
—Sahih Muslim and Sahih al-Bukhari

He is a man of medium height; *of a ruddy, fair complexion;* will be dressed in two pieces of dyed garment; and the hair of his head will appear as if water is trickling out of it, although it will not be wet.
—Ahmad ibn Hanbal, Musnad

He has curly red hair and wide shoulders. He will break the cross and abolish the jizya, and accept no other religion but Islam ... [In his time] Nothing and nobody but God will be worshipped. He will practice Muhammad's law and belong to Muhammad's people. He will follow the Prophet even though he himself is a Prophet, because he saw him [Mahammed] on the night of Mi`raj. Therefore, he [Jesus] will be the most distinguished Companion.

—Jalaluddin as-Suyuti, Nuzul `Isa ibn Maryam Akhir al-Zaman, 182

While sleeping near the Ka'bah last night, I [Muhammad] saw in my dream *a man of brown color the best one can see among those who are brown colored*, and his long hair fell between his shoulders. His hair was lank, water dribbled from his head, and he was placing his hands on the shoulders of two men while circumambulating the Ka'bah. I asked: "Who is this?" They replied, "This is Jesus, son of Mary."

—Sahih al-Bukhari

While not all of these Islamic descriptions of Jesus are in perfect agreement, we can see that the most common description of Jesus is that of a ruddy Jesus with red curly hair. All of the Islamic traditions are very important due to the fact that roughly 1.8 billion Muslims ascribe much weight to the descriptions and anticipate Jesus' arrival to fulfill these prophecies and ultimately to carry out all of the above-described atrocities. And secondly, these physical descriptions are relevant due to the fact that they are drastically different from that which has been received by the Church primarily through iconography—traditional images of Jesus passed on from generation to generation—but particularly for the sake of this discussion, in St. Faustina's Image. So as a very large portion of the religious population of the world anticipates the arrival of Jesus as a Muslim who will essentially annul the Christian conception of Jesus and abolish all other religions, much of the Christian world remains unaware of the description that Christ Himself presented to St. Faustina. Therefore, the mystery now arrives here: Two Jesuses, two descriptions, and an Image that Pope John Paul II believed was of vital importance for all of humanity to see. There is yet another mysterious element to this story which involves the vision of a young woman in Spain who was given a message that she would one day have to alert the World's media concerning a mystical event the entire world would witness. As a child she was taken to share her story with the Vatican. The event is speculated to be a miracle the whole world will witness!

Chapter Twenty

Fatima, Medjugorge, and Garabandal

Sightings of the Virgin Mary may seem as preposterous to the non-believer as the non-believers appear to people of faith. However, whatever your own particular thoughts on this matter, what is known is that these so called sightings of the Mother of God have become more common place in recent times. An editorial that appeared in the Catholic weekly *America*, describes the unexplainable phenomenon this way:

Few indeed are those who... are present as eyewitnesses of one of those rare but terribly real occurrences in which the omnipotence of God strikes through the shadows of time and space to bind up and heal the broken lives of men. However, the evidence of these visitations is indisputable. During the last century it has pleased God so to visit His people time after time at a remote grotto in the French foothills of the Pyrenees, where the Blessed Virgin Mother of God appeared in 1858 to little Bernadette Soubirous. God of course chooses His own times and places and occasions for the miraculous, but His power shines forth most frequently where His Mother is honored and venerated.

Today, millions of pilgrims, many of whom are sick and dying go to Lourdes. Located in the French Pyrenees, it is a place where worshippers truly believe a young peasant girl was visited by the Virgin Mary, and where water from the grotto where the young girl claimed to have seen her has miraculous healing power. These people are also keen to learn more about Bernadette, a young girl who fought such a fearless fight for the authenticity of her visions to be believed.

An innocent and simple maiden, quite similar in many ways to Faustina, Bernadette was given the grace and strength to convince Church authorities of the messages she received at Lourdes. Hers was a Herculean task and it was not hard to see why in 1858, and aged only fourteen, her apparitions were not taken seriously.

So great was her conviction however, that at 22 Bernadette vowed to give her life to God and entered the Convent in Nevers. It was a hard life and one made none the easier by her Superior who could not believe the stories of her visions. As a result Bernadette was driven hard, and nearly died in the year of her entry yet she would continue to live a life of service without complaint, and chose instead to inspire others. Four years later after becoming a nun and while tending the war wounded in the hospital in Nevers, Bernadette left behind a trail of laughter and of ease. In the last two years of her life, and plagued by illness Bernadette's body became a mere shadow of its former self; and she died at age 35.

Today, Bernadette's body remains incorrupt and is laid in a glass reliquary in the Convent of St. Gildarde in Nevers. It is interesting to note that usually death extinguishes a human face in the twinkling of an eye, but in this instance death illuminated the face of Bernadette.

In some ways Divine intervention seemed to play a role in enabling us to know anything about Bernadette Soubirous and one man namely, Franz Werfel, would help bring her story to the world. Werfel was a German-speaking Jew born in Prague in 1890, and became a well-known and gifted playwright. Tragically however, like so many millions of others, the Nazi regime would change his life.

The story is best described by Werfel himself in his Personal Preface to The Song of Bernadette:

"In the last days of June 1940, in flight after the collapse of France, the two of us, my wife and I, had hoped to elude our mortal enemies in time to cross the Spanish frontier to Portugal, but had to flee back to the interior of France on the very night German troops occupied the frontier town of Hendaye. The Pyrenean departments had turned into a phantasmagoria—a very camp of chaos.

The Werfel's joined thousands of refugees who wandered the roads obstructing towns and villages: Frenchmen, Belgians, Dutchmen, Poles, Czechs, Austrians, exiled Germans, and, mingled with these, soldiers of the defeated armies. There was barely food enough to still the extreme pangs of hunger. There was no shelter to be had. Anyone who had obtained possession of an upholstered chair for his night's rest was an object of envy. In endless lines, stood the cars of the fugitives, piled high with household gear, with mattresses and beds. There was no petrol to be had.

"A family settled in Pau told us that Lourdes was the one place where, if luck were kind, one might find a roof. Since Lourdes was but thirty kilometers distant, we were advised to make the attempt and knock on its gates. We followed this advice and found refuge at last in the little town of Lourdes in the foothills of the Pyrenees."

It was there, in her native town, that Franz Werfel became acquainted with the strange and beautiful story of Bernadette Soubirous, the young peasant girl who from February to July 1858 reported eighteen visions of the Blessed Virgin Mary. Hunted by the Gestapo throughout the Werfel's stay in Lourdes, they experienced excruciating anxiety, not just for themselves but for their hosts. In the Werfels' desperate situation, a number of families courageously came forward, taking turns in giving them shelter, and from those families they heard about the moving events and the miraculous healings of Lourdes.

Werfel vowed that, if he and his wife survived their desperate situation, he would put off all other tasks and 'sing', as best he could, 'the song of Bernadette'.

After many tribulations, the Werfels reached the safety of America and true to his word Werfel wrote The Song of Bernadette, a novel which tells the story of Saint Bernadette Soubirous. The book was published in 1942 and was extremely popular, spending more than a year on the New York Times Best Seller list and 13 weeks atop the list.

In Franz Werfel's own words: 'This book is the fulfillment of my vow.' As a result of that vow, Werfel's novel would become a film, and receive an Academy award. Werfel died in 1945 and the Cardinal Archbishop of Los Angeles, having obtained the family's permission, gave him a Christian burial. After the war, Franz Werfel was re-buried in Vienna.

Subsequent to Lourdes, there have been repeated apparitions, each one of which seemed to warn of some impending disaster for the world and inform us that we might be on the verge of destruction. Some of these sightings have yet to receive official authentication from the Church, and we know that the inner sanctum of the Vatican views each apparition with great caution. In fact, far from welcoming a sighting of the Mother of God, it treats such matters from a position of deep skepticism.

However most will agree that there is increasing evidence to suggest that modern day society needs to take a closer look at our world. Sadly while we now live at a time when all things seem technologically possible, there is a reality that we are now somewhat uncertain about what will the future bring. These sightings are in effect meant to remind earth of the existence of heaven.

Probably the most famous of all the apparitions in the 20th Century was Fatima where The Blessed Virgin Mary, the Mother of God, appeared 6 times to 3 shepherd children; Lucy, Francisco and Jacinta; between May 13 and October 13, 1917. Mary came to the little village in Portugal. which historically had remained faithful to the Catholic Church. However, at the time of this apparition, the New Republic was against the church and it was a very troubled period in Portuguese history. In fact, when the Blessed Mother came to that country in 1917, Portugal was in a state of complete turmoil: "Economic failure, aggravated still more by the recent entrance into the war, disorder and anarchy, dissensions and murders, assassination attempts which had become everyday occurrences – all these created the atmosphere of a real civil war. The Church had been banned from society, reduced to silence, persecuted in every way. In short, Portugal in that hour experienced the darkest period of its history."

Not surprisingly, sightings of the Virgin Mary were the last thing this anti clerical government wanted but they could do nothing to stop them or to stop the thousands of pilgrims who flocked to Fatima upon hearing news of the sightings. In each instance Our Lady came with a message from God to every man, woman and child of our century. Our Lady of Fatima promised that the whole world would be in peace, and that many souls would go to Heaven if Her requests were listened to and obeyed. She told us that war is a punishment for sin; that God would punish the world for its sins in our time by means of war, hunger, persecution of the

Church and persecution of the Pope, unless we listened to and obeyed the command of God.

Further intrigue from these apparitions at Fatima was provided by the existence of three envelopes, the third of which was believed to have contained the prediction of Pope John Paul II's assassination attempt. The letter was opened eighteen years after the attempt on the Pontiff's life and the contents revealed to the public in Vatican City, June 26, 2000 when the Holy See Press Office, presented the document "The Message of Fatima." It had been prepared by the Congregation for the Doctrine of the Faith and it carries the signatures of Cardinal Joseph Ratzinger and Archbishop Tarcisio Bertone S.D.B., respectively prefect and secretary of the congregation. The document, over 40 pages long, was published in English, French, Italian, Spanish, German, Portuguese, and Polish and contained Sister Lucy's third letter.

It is very interesting to note the content.

> *After the two parts which I have already explained, at the left of Our Lady and a little above, we saw an Angel with a flaming sword in his left hand; flashing, it gave out flames that looked as though they would set the world on fire; but they died out in contact with the splendor that Our Lady radiated towards him from her right hand: Pointing to the earth with his right hand, the Angel cried out in a loud voice: 'Penance, Penance, Penance!'. And we saw in an immense light that is God: 'something similar to how people appear in a mirror when they pass in front of it a Bishop dressed in White,' we had the impression that it was the Holy Father. Other Bishops, Priests, men and women Religious were going up a steep mountain, at the top of which there was a big Cross of rough-hewn trunks as of a cork-tree with the bark; before reaching there, the Holy Father passed through a big city, half in ruins and half trembling with halting step, afflicted with pain and sorrow, he prayed for the souls of the corpses he met on his way; having reached the top of the mountain, on his knees at the foot of the big Cross he was killed by a group of soldiers who fired bullets and arrows at him, and in the same way there died one after another the other Bishops, Priests, men and women Religious, and*

various lay people of different ranks and positions. Beneath the two arms of the Cross there were two Angels each with a crystal aspersorium in his hand, in which they gathered up the blood of the Martyrs and with it sprinkled the souls that were making their way to God."

Specifically the text suggests a killing and not a failed assassination attempt, and therefore some are still not fully convinced that this prophecy has been fulfilled.

However, there can be no denying that it was on The Feast of Our Lady of Fatima when something unquestionably miraculous happened in St Peter's Square. It was the day that an assassin attempted—and failed— to kill Pope John Paul II. The Pope has expressed that it was indeed the Mother of God that saved his life. Even Ali Agca, the Pope's would - be assassin was fascinated by Fatima and when Pope John Paul II went to visit him in jail and forgave him, the man who could have ended the Pontiff's life asked about Fatima. As John Paul recalled:

Around Christmas 1983 I visited my attacker in prison. We spoke at length. Ali Agca, as everyone knows was a professional assassin. This means the attack was not of his own initiative, it was someone else's idea; someone else had commissioned him to carry it out. In the course of conversation it became clear that Ali Agca was still wondering how the attempted assassination could possibly have failed. He had planned it meticulously, attending to every tiny detail. Yet his intended victim had escaped death. How could this have happened? The interesting thing was that his perplexity had led him to the religious question. He wanted to know about the secret of Fatima, and what the secret actually was. This was his principal concern; more than anything else, he wanted to know this. Perhaps those insistent questions showed that he had grasped something really important. Ali Agca had probably sensed that over and above his own power, over and above the power of shooting and killing, there was a higher power. He then began to look for it. I hope and pray that he found it.

Over the years millions of pilgrims have gone to Fatima to connect to the place that they believe was visited by the Virgin Mary. There have also been countless reports of other sightings of the Blessed Mother in all corners of the world. From Our Lady of Akita in Japan the city which is interestingly in close proximity to North Korea. Then there is Our Lady of Guadalupe's appearance in Mexico, along with sightings close to Bosnia, as well as Garabandal in Spain. Yet, while some of these sightings have received the endorsement of the Church, others have not. However, there is one apparition that stands out from the others, and while not yet approved by the Vatican, it has not been either denied or disaffirmed. Indeed, the story of the sightings at Garabandal is particularly interesting because it includes an eight day warning and a worldwide media press call!

Again, just like Lourdes, and Fatima this sighting took place in a most unlikely location. San Sebastian de Garabandal is a small hamlet of some 80 humble dwellings in the Cantabrian Mountains of northwest Spain. According to accounts, it was here that from June 1, 1961, to November 13, 1965, the Blessed Virgin appeared to four young girls from the village. Furthermore, during this four-year period, an extraordinary number of apparitions occurred in fact, more than 2000—and with some lasting a few hours.

The four girls: Conchita Gonzales (the principal spokesperson with the Blessed Virgin); Mari Loli Mazon, Jacinta Gonzalez; and Mari Cruz Gonzalez were eleven and twelve years old at the time. Today, three of the four visionaries have married Americans and live in the United States. They lead exemplary Christian lives, totally dedicated to their vocations as wives and mothers. Conchita has four children, Mari Loli three and Jacinta one. Mari Cruz is also married, living in Spain and has four children. As the story of Garbandal has been recounted, the girls were apparently playing on the outskirts of the village when they heard a sound like thunder. Suddenly, according to their testimonies, there stood before them a dazzling angel. He said nothing and quickly disappeared. Pale and visibly shaken, the girls ran to the village church and relayed their story concerning the apparition. Over the next twelve days the angel appeared to them several more times. Then on July 1, he spoke for the first time announcing that on the following day, The Blessed Virgin would appear to them as Our Lady of Mount Carmel. News spread quickly. On July 2, many priests were among the numerous visitors who joined the villagers to witness the great event. At about 6:00 p.m., the children were headed for the spot where they had been seeing the angel when the Blessed Virgin appeared with an angel on each side. They recognized one of the angels as the one who had been appearing to them (later identified as St. Michael the Archangel) and the other looked identical. Above the Virgin was a large eye that the children thought to be the eye of God. They spoke openly and familiarly with their Heavenly Mother and said the rosary in her presence. Over the next year and a half, she would appear hundreds of times several times in a single day. These are the contents of the Virgin Mary's messages:

October 18, 1961:

> We must make many sacrifices, perform much penance, and visit the Blessed Sacrament frequently. But first, we must lead good lives. If we do not, a Chastisement will befall us. The cup is already filling up and if we do not change, a very great Chastisement will come upon us.

JUNE 18, 1965:

> As my message of October 18 has not been complied with and has not been made known to the world, I am advising you that this is the last one. Before, the cup was filling up. Now it is flowing over. Many cardinals, many bishops, and many priests are on the road to perdition and are taking many souls with them. Less and less importance is being given to the Eucharist. You should turn the wrath of God away from yourselves by your efforts. If you ask His forgiveness with sincere hearts, He will pardon you. I, your mother, through the intercession of Saint Michael the Archangel, ask you to amend your lives. You are now receiving the last warnings. I love you very much and do not want your condemnation. Pray to us with sincerity and we will grant your requests. You should make more sacrifices. Think about the passion of Jesus.

Three great supernatural events were also prophesied at Garabandal. The first is a worldwide warning from God to be seen and then felt interiorly by everyone on earth. At that moment, we will see the wrong we've done and the good we failed to do. *The Warning* will be sent to correct the conscience of the world and prepare it for *The Great Miracle*. This is how the witnesses describe what will happen:

Conchita Gonzalez' Diary, June 2, 1965:

This warning, like the chastisement, is a very fearful thing for the good as well as the wicked. It will draw the good closer to God and it will warn the wicked that the end of time [not to be confused with the end of the world] is coming and that these are the last warnings. No one can stop it from happening. It is certain, although I know nothing of the day or the date. The warning will be like a revelation of our sins, and it will be seen and experienced equally by believers and non-believers and people of all religions. Each person on earth will have an interior experience of how they stand in the light of God's Justice. It is like purification for the miracle. And it is like a catastrophe. It will make us think of the dead, that is, we would prefer to be dead than to experience the warning. Jesus will send the warning to purify us so that we may better appreciate the miracle by which he clearly proves his love for us and hence his desire that we see the consequences of the sins we have committed. I think that those who do not despair will experience great good from it for their sanctification. The warning is something supernatural and will not be explained by science. It will be seen and experienced by all men all over the world and will be a direct work of God. It will be very awesome. However, if men die from it, it will be only from the emotional shock of seeing it. It will be a correction of the conscience of the world. Those who do not know Christ (non-Christians) will believe it is a warning from God.

While one of the other children, Jacinta, describing the warning has said;

The Warning is something that is seen in the air, everywhere in the world and is immediately transmitted into the interior of our souls.

It will last a very little time, but it will seem a very long time because of its effect within us. It would be like fire. It will not burn our flesh, but we will feel it bodily and interiorly.

156

She goes on to describe astronomical phenomena:

> **Like two stars—that crash and make a lot of noise,
> and a lot of light—but they don't fall. It's not going to hurt
> us but we're going to see it and, in that moment, we're going
> to see our consciences.**

In addition to these events, Conchita has stated that she was told by the Blessed Virgin in 1962 that after the death of Pope John XXIII,

> **"There would be two more popes after Pope Paul VI
> and that one of the popes would have a very short reign…
> After that would come the end-times but not the end of
> the world."**

If Conchita has interpreted this vision of Mary correctly, then Pope John Paul II have been the last of the popes before the end times begin. This is one possible explanation for the timing of his death on the eve of Divine Mercy just moments after celebrating the vigil Mass.

Conchita said that she has been given the date of the Miracle by the Blessed Virgin and will announce the date to the world's media eight days before it is to occur. Since The Miracle will occur after The Warning, it is highly likely that both The Warning and The Miracle will occur within the next thirty years given Conchita is presently in her fifties. That is of course if this apparition is valid. Conchita has also said in her Diary,

> **I am the only one to whom the Blessed Virgin spoke
> of the miracle. She forbade me to say what it will consist
> of. I can't announce the date either until eight days before
> it is due to occur. What I can reveal is that it will coincide
> with an event in the Church and with the feast of a saint,
> martyr of the Eucharist; that it will take place at 8:30 on
> a Thursday evening; that it will be visible to all those who
> are in the village and surrounding the mountains; that the
> sick who are present will be cured, and the incredulous
> will believe. It will be the greatest miracle that Jesus will
> have performed for the world. There won't be the slightest
> doubt that it comes from God and that it is for the good of
> mankind.**

On September 14, 1965, Conchita said, **"The sign that will remain forever at the pines is something we will be able to photograph, televise, and see, but not touch. It will be evident that it is not a thing of this world but from God."** At another time, concerning the great miracle she added, **"It would last about 15 minutes."** On August 10, 1971, while talking to a group of Americans, she offered this revealing information: **"It will take place on or between the eighth and sixteenth of March, April, or May. It will not happen in February or June."** Eight days in advance of *The Miracle*, Conchita will give notice to the world about its coming. Prior to the eight-day notice, God will send a warning to the entire world to purify it for the great miracle. Therefore, the world will receive two advance notices: *The Warning* and the eight-day notice.

What makes Concita's prophecy so interesting is that by definition, in order to warn the media, she has to be alive. Will this visible sign be a real image of Divine Mercy? What is known is that this woman is a much-loved figure within the Church and has been listened to by Popes and mystics within Vatican circles. In addition, while the Church has yet to endorse Garabandal, there may be some valid reasons why it has not. Mari-Loli Mazon meanwhile knows the year of The Warning.

So could *The Image of Divine Mercy*, the Image that matches the Shroud be the Image that we may one-day witness in the sky? We have two situations developing, an Image Christ wanted painted to prepare the world for His final coming and an anticipated warning given to a young girl in Garabandal Spain many years ago. We also have Chapter 13 of Revelation which we will soon examine as the possible reason for *The Warning* and *The Image*. Yet for the moment the question remains: Why did Christ want this Image known to all mankind and why unlike all the other visionaries and seers throughout this past century was Faustina the one who became a Saint with such a historical and prominent emphasis— the first Saint of the 21st Century?

CHAPTER TWENTY ONE

FAUSTINA'S DIARY AND ITS MESSAGE FOR US TODAY

In one of her apparitions Jesus said to Sister Faustina:

> *"Know that your task is to write down everything that I make known to you about My mercy, for the benefit of those who by reading these things will be comforted in their souls and will have the courage to approach Me"*
>
> **—Diary entry 1693**

Today the Vatican believes that in an extraordinary way, *The Diary*, "delights not only the simple and uneducated people, but also scholars who look upon it as an additional source of Theo-logical research." Thus far *The Diary* has been translated into many languages, including, English, German, Italian, Spanish, French, Portuguese, Arabic, Russian, Hungarian, Czech, and Slovak and has sold over five hundred thousand copies worldwide. Yet it is only now just a few years after Faustina's canonization that we can truly begin to see the fruits of this mystical puzzle unfold before us. Is this all part of the Divine timetable?

Throughout biblical and Church history, God has always shown himself to be a self-revealing God—He is the God who speaks. As such, He has always sent messages at various times of need, when troubles seemed to overwhelm the world. Would it then be appropriate in light of the present world situation, that He would send messages to mankind now? Are we not in need of some divine reassurance? Whether one lives in America, England, Europe, or the Middle East, are we not now all at an impasse? Who among us is able to state with confidence that the future of our world is bright? Who among us is not somewhat fearful of what the future may hold? The uncertainly of the future has made us all a bit uneasy. Whether one is Catholic or Protestant, Jewish, Hindu, Buddhist, Muslim—whether religious or agnostic, should we not at least pause to consider the messages that have been so thoroughly endorsed by Pope John Paul II, one of the holiest and most adored men of the last hundred years? Should not the great emphasis that the most traveled Pope in history placed on this message give us good reason to ponder its meaning? John Paul believed Christ had instructed Faustina to let the "**Whole World**" have access to the *the Image* and *the Diary*, and tried within his papacy to bring attention to both. Should we not all then at least make an effort to become familiar with these divinely inspired works in light of all that is happening around us?

Let us also not forget the passenger who prayed to St Faustina, as his flight made a miraculous landing on New York's Hudson River, or the Multiple Scherosis sufferer who walked after praying in front of the Image.

Today, we live in a world that is more message friendly than any previous generation. Every day, we are bombarded by hundreds, if not thousands, of messages. We have become societies reliant on texting and e-mails. Hardly any area of the world is exempt from the ringing of cell phones or the pinging of Blackberries. We are indeed, a message friendly people. Yet more recently, specifically since the horror of 9-11, we have also been subjected to regular messages of a very sinister nature—dark messages, prophecies and warnings sent to us from an obscure safe house or cave in an undisclosed location—or more recently, from the very Presidential Palace of Iran. In all these cases, the messages seem to come from some enigmatic character that seems to be larger than life. The messages are most often messages of rebuke, promises of divine chastisement, divine retribution, punishment, revenge, hatred, and hopelessness. There are also messages being delivered by fundamentalist Imans at Mosques throughout the world, calling for an Islamic take over on a global scale at all costs and no matter the consequences. Yet when we really think about it these messages often filled with hate for the so called 'infidel' are the polar opposite to Christ's messages imparted to Faustina promise; ***"Do not fear anything; I am always with you."*** Diary entry 613

Now let us also further consider the messages we have been receiving over the past five years from a man who has no location, who lives at large but who intermittently reaches out to the world with His messages of fear and hatred. There is a bounty on his head but the West has apparently yet to find Osama Bin Laden. Nonetheless his chilling and terrifying threats still reach our homes. Threats such as his message to his brothers in Pakistan on September 24, 2001;

We urge these brothers to be considered the first martyrs in the battle of Islam against the neo-crusader-Jewish campaign led by Bush, the biggest crusader, under the banner of the cross. This battle can be seen as merely one of the battles of eternal Islam.

By using such loaded religious language; "neo-crusader-Jewish campaign", "under the banner of the cross", Bin Laden is purposefully conjuring up both the painful history of the crusades, as well as a strictly religious world where all Jews and Christians continually live to conspire together against all Muslims. This worldview derives from the Quran itself:

> *O you who believe! Take not the Jews and the Christians as friends; they are but friends of each other. And whoever befriends them, then surely, he is one of them.*
>
> **—Quran 5:51**

Such is Bin Laden's belief that he even referred to 9/11 as "These blessed, successful strikes." In fact Bin Laden has been a messenger of hate whose cryptic messages have dominated the news since the turn of this Century.

Sadly, many people still believe that radical Islam's war against Jews is due to the presence of the Nation of Israel in the Middle East. However, centuries before Israel as a Nation ever existed, Muhammad's prophecies declared that Muslims must slaughter all Jews before the Utopian Muslim age may commence has been well known by faithful Muslims. The tradition reads as follows:

[Muhammad said:] The last hour would not come unless the Muslims will fight against the Jews and the Muslims would kill them until the Jews would hide themselves behind a stone or a tree and a stone or a tree would say: Muslim or the servant of Allah, there is a Jew behind me; come and kill him.

—Sahih Muslim 41:6985

In other words, the radical apocalyptic minded Muslims like Bin Laden believe that they will never see this prophesied Golden Age of Islam until they completely defeat and slaughter all Jews. As such, anyone who supports the Nation of Israel is on Bin Laden's list.

Let us also remember that every day in every way, al-Qaeda reiterates through their messages that its target is not only all " infidels," including Jews, Christians, Buddhists, and Hindus, but also what the radicals refer to as "the hypocrites". There are the vast majority of the world's moderate Muslims, who reject the extremists' vision of a restored Caliphate. In one of Bin Laden's tapes, aimed at Muslims, he described his enemy as "the Romans . . . gathered under the banner of the cross," but it also denounced Muslim "infidels and heretics."

The point that we are trying to emphasize here is that the present Jihad being waged by various radicals such as Bin Laden is not strictly being waged against Christians and Jews or Westerners. Moderate Muslims from all over the world are most certainly being targeted as well. Could this be another reason why Faustina was sent these messages of hope for *"all mankind"*? For it seems that each and every one of us is in need of the message of God's love, as found in Faustina's revelations.

It is interesting to note that among the many things that John Paul II wrote about in his last book, *Memory and Identity* concerning of the historical truth about Israel.

Israel, as God's chosen people, was a theocratic society, in which Moses was not only the charismatic leader but also the prophet. His task, in God's name, was to build the juridical and religious foundations for the people's common life. A key moment in this work was the event which took place at the foot of Mount Sinai. There, the Covenant was established between God and the people of Israel on the basis of the law given by God to Moses on the mountain.

The Pope was of course referring to The Ten Commandments, but he also reaffirms that far from being merely a product of political agenda, the very land of Israel was given at the foot of Mount Sinai to the Jews by God. Yet the Iranian President Mahmoud Ahmadinejad and Osama Bin Laden seem determined to ignore this historical reality and instead focus on fulfilling the prophecy about a final holocaust. As a result the messages we are receiving from them and their followers reiterate hatred for and elimination of the Jewish and Christian believers.

Then there are the threats from various terrorist organizations such as Hamas and Hezbollah, along with statements from the Iranian President concerning the annihilation of Israel and a world without America. While the world seems to be hurling toward a much darker day, we cannot but believe that there is an alternative to all of the fear and hopelessness that seems to be crashing down like one wave after another. *Good must rise from evil.*

On September 18th, 2006 came the most chilling threat of all when Al-Qaeda in Iraq citing remarks by Pope Benedict XVI linking Islam with violence, said it would wage jihad until the West is defeated. "We say to the servant of the cross (the Pope): wait for defeat ... We say to infidels and tyrants: wait for what will afflict you." "We continue our jihad. We will not stop until the banner of unicity flies throughout the world," read the statement attributed to the Mujahideen consultative council. "We will smash the cross ... (you will have no choice but) Islam or death," the statement added, citing a hadith (saying of the Prophet Muhammad) promising Muslims they would "conquer Rome ... as they conquered Constantinople."

Anyone who still believes this is not a holy war is very much mistaken,

Whichever way we look at it, the world is engaged in a clash between good, and evil, but, also in a showdown where the jihadists are exhibiting global terror. Now, we have to truly ask ourselves whether God would really allow the world to be utterly destroyed unless it conformed to Islam? Therefore, does it not stand to reason that at a time when we are confronted with such an overwhelming tide of evil, that God would have also arranged the arrival of an another message—a message of hope and mercy? Could Faustina's messages be a clear reminder that God is indeed present and watching over all of us? Could *Faustina's Diary* and messages be calling us all, despite the daily terror that we face, to indeed take heed to the inscription on The Divine Mercy Image: *"Jesus I trust in You."*

It is indeed a terrifying juncture in history—perhaps one that we do not yet understand the full extent of. While any suggestion that *"The End is Nigh"* will be met by most with scoffs, world events in 2006, such as the clash of Hezbollah and Israel do seem to correlate in an astounding way to the chapters of The Book of Revelation and the various eschatological prophecies of the Bible.

Consider this: In the Book of the Prophet Ezekiel, chapter 38, we read about a coalition of nations that is said to attack the Nation of Israel in the last days. Among the nations that are listed are the following: Turkey, Iran, Syria, Sudan, Libya, and "many nations with [them]". The prophecy reads eerily similar to what we see today in the Nation of Israel and the Middle East. Speaking to the leader of these last-days, anti-Israel coalition, God says the following:

> *In future years you will invade a land that has recovered from war, whose people were gathered from many nations to the mountains of Israel, which had long been desolate. They had been brought out from the nations, and now all of them live in safety. You and all your troops and the many nations with you will go up, advancing like a storm; you will be like a cloud covering the land.*
>
> —Ezekiel 38:8, 9

Therefore, it's quite eerie indeed to see the very political alliances that the Bible portrays are existing in the last-days, being nearly present in the Middle East today.

Adding to all of this is the possibility that within our lifetime we may indeed witness that which Pope John Paul II warned us of; namely the use of atomic stockpiles.

While seemingly every society has had those who believed that they were living in the end-times, never before have world events seemed to be leaning so close to biblical prophecy. Certainly this would explain why Christ instructed Faustina to *"Prepare the world for My final coming."*

(Diary entry 429) In our world rife with struggle and suffering it is sometimes difficult to remember that we are governed by a stronger more powerful force, a higher power. A force that once visited a humble nun called Faustina offering words of peace and hope for all mankind. As Faustina was instructed in the Diary,

> *"O soul steeped in darkness, do not despair. All is not yet lost. Come and confide in your God, who is love and mercy."*

—Diary entry 1486

We live in a world where many are left asking how God can allow disasters to happen? However, we must remember that in God's time a thousand years is but one day. Indeed, if we can believe this, our struggles, though while appearing to last forever, are in fact not even seconds in the eternal plan.

Similarly, the theme of the image, given to Faustina, which God wants the world to see represents the risen savior who brings peace and love to all people. It is an invitation to "Trust in Him" when all else fails.

> *"My child, make the resolution never to rely on people. Entrust yourself completely to My will saying, "Not as I want, but according to your will, O God, let it be done unto me. These words spoken from the heart, can raise a soul to the summit of sanctity in a short time."*

—Diary entry 1487

Among the promises that Christ assured Faustina of was the grace of a happy death for all who prayerfully meditate on this image.

> *"By means of this image I shall grant many graces to souls; so let every soul have access to it.*

—Diary entry 570

As Jesus told Faustina, it was not in the brush strokes on the canvas *but in the grace,* adding to the conclusion that this image of Divine Mercy was not just a painting but also an actual vessel which people should pay attention to. As we have seen, Jesus also expressed His desire that people would participate in the Feast of Divine Mercy—a day in Church history which was traditionally when this world and the next converge: The eighth day of the octave of Easter.

It is interesting to note that in the celebration of Hanukah the eighth day is also significant. It is the day when the candle burns the brightest on the Menorah again because of the convergence of this life and the next.

It was of course on the eve of the feast of Mercy when Pope John Paul II left this earth only moments after receiving Communion. A fitting departure for the man who had sanctioned the occasion in the Church for as Christ had once stated;

> *"Whatever soul will go to confession and receive Holy communion on that day will obtain complete forgiveness of sins and punishment. On that day are open all the divine floodgates, through which graces flow. Let no soul fear to draw near to me, even though its sins be as scarlet."*
>
> **—Diary entry 699**

Just as a simple Polish nun defied all odds and carried out Christ's mission to complete the Image and instate the prayer, we can also be assured of hope in the prayer which Christ wanted recited at three in the afternoon. It is a prayer that was meant to be directed to Him which offers this promise:

> *"In this hour I will refuse nothing to the soul that makes a request of Me in virtue of My Passion… In this hour you can obtain anything for yourself and for others, for the asking; it was the hour of grace for the whole world: mercy triumphed over justice." — Diary entry 1572*

At this juncture in world history, regardless of what belief system you adhere to, surely a prayer offering mercy for even the most hardened sinner is a gift we can only benefit from, and certainly we have nothing to lose. And so in reading this book, you have become aware of the promise of mercy, and hopefully despite what is happening in the world can be reassured that when all else seems to fail we can "Trust in Him."

In the Bible, in the Old Testament, we are given stories recounting the communications of God with those individuals He chose to impart messages to. In the New Testament we witness the story of Christ's birth in the nativity in Bethlehem, His ministry on earth, His miracles, His death, burial, and resurrection. Then centuries later we had *The Shroud*; a linen cloth many believe is the actual burial sheet of Christ. Now years later, following the authentication of *The Shroud* based on scientific studies, we have *The Image of Divine Mercy*: The Image which Christ instructed Faustina to have painted is a perfect match to *The Shroud*. Are these conceivably physical proofs, each standing two thousand years apart, both matching, both identical, both bearing testimony to His existence and providing living proof and encouragement for all to place their "Trust in Him"? Faustina stated that there was one thing that separated her from every other angel or Saint and everyone that ever lived. If indeed it is direct knowledge of the end of the world, the one man on earth who may have been closest to God, Pope John Paul II, believed her. Is it not possible that out of every living soul, the late Pontiff would have been one to know?

The full extent of John Paul's II gift to the world may still not be fully realized but we do know that he was a unique, humble and holy man who truly imitated Christ and embraced the world. Yet above all he was human and made us feel close to him.

His was a papacy made for the age of air miles. "The Pope can't remain a prisoner in the Vatican," he once said. "I want to go to everybody ... from the nomads in the steppes to the monks and nuns in their convents ... I want to cross the threshold of every home." And so he did. He also wanted to bring Faustina's messages to every home as well.

In conducting the research for this book and concerned about the fanatical element within Islam which is clearly killing people of every belief system, including Muslims themselves, we turned to history to look at another point in time when fanaticism also threatened the freedom of the world. While back in the 1930's there were those warning of impending doom very few seemed to listen

For it is interesting to recall that Adolf Hitler had one strange bedfellow whose beliefs concerning Israel and Jews bear a chilling parallel to the current President of Iran and the membership of Al Qaeda.

Muhammad Amin al-Husseini, the uncle of Yassar Arafat, was born somewhere between 1893 and 1895. Amin was the son of the Mufti of Jerusalem, and member of an esteemed, aristocratic family. The Husseinis were one of the richest and most powerful of all the rivaling clans in the Ottoman province known as the Judaean part of Palestine.

Just one year before Faustina's death in 1937, the Grand Mufti expressed his solidarity with Germany, asking the Nazi Third Reich to oppose establishment of a Jewish state, stop Jewish immigration to Palestine, and provide arms to the Arab population...

According to documentation from the Nuremberg and Eichmann trials, the Nazi Germany SS helped finance al-Husseini's efforts in the 1936-39 revolt in Palestine. Adolf Eichmann actually visited Palestine and met with al-Husseini at that time and subsequently maintained regular contact with him later in Berlin.

Further confirmation of his friendship with Hitler was provided at the Nuremberg Trials, where Eichmann's deputy Dieter Wisliceny (subsequently executed as a war criminal) testified:

The Mufti was one of the initiators of the systematic extermination of European Jewry and had been a collaborator and adviser of Eichmann and Himmler in the execution of this plan. ... He was one of Eichmann's best friends and had constantly incited him to accelerate the extermination measures. I heard him say, accompanied by Eichmann, he had visited incognito the gas chamber of Auschwitz.

Haj Amin al-Husseini eventually died in exile in 1974. His place as leader of the radical, nationalist Palestinian Arabs was taken by his nephew MuhammadAbdel-Raouf Arafat As Qudwa al-Hussaeini, better known as Yaaser Arafat. In August 2002, Arafat gave an interview in which he referred to "our hero al-Husseini" as a symbol of Palestinian Arab resistance. Clearly we must see that history should not repeat itself. We should also be aware that the hand fundamentalist Islam played with the third Reich.

At the conclusion of our findings between *The Image* and the possibility of a false Messiah, and a sweep of radical religious terror across the world, we presented our research to a Scripture expert. We were referred to Chapter 13 of the Book of Revelation which concerns the coming of a false image. The image of the beast, the anti-Christ, stands in direct opposition to the Image of Christ Jesus imparted to Faustina.

> *The [second] beast told them to build an image in honor of the [first] beast that had been wounded by the sword yet lived. The second beast was allowed to breathe life into the image of the first beast, so that the image could talk and put to death all those who would not worship it. The beast forced all people, small and great, rich and poor, slave and free, to have a mark placed on their right hands or their foreheads. No one could buy or sell without having this mark, that is, the beast's name, or the number that stands for the name. This calls for wisdom. Whoever is intelligent can work out the meaning of the number of the beast, because the number stands for a human name. Its number is 666.*
>
> **—Revelation 13:14-18**

While it can be asked if, the Divine Mercy image is the face of the coming Messiah, why it is not universally known? The only possible explanation is Divine intervention playing a role. Could it be because it was not the right time to reveal its true significance before? Did Pope John Paul II do everything he could to bring Saint Faustina and her messages to the world, at a juncture in history when the world was on the verge of a spiritual confrontation and might better understand it? In the pages of this book we have discovered how the late Pontiff, not only made Faustina the first saint of this century but even died after celebrating the vigil Mass installed because of what Faustina had been told decades before. Yet, why was John Paul II the only Pope to pay so much attention to it. The only Vicar of Christ who based his whole Pontificate on these messages? Did no one else understand it?

In truth Saint Faustina and her messages were taken seriously before. In fact the message of Divine Mercy was actually first written about in a book entitled *Mercy is Forever* by Fr. Theodore Zaremba, O.F.M. First published in 1957 by the Franciscan Fathers of the Assumption Province, headquartered in Pulaski, Wisconsin. The book was reprinted in 1979, touched on the importance and significance of Saint Faustina, and the Image and message Christ had imparted to her. According to Zaremba, Vatican Radio mentioned the devotion a number of times. In fact, on February 24, 1948, there was a special broadcast entitled "Sister Faustina, the Apostle of the Mercy of God." It talked about her life and "mentioned that Jesus was pleased with her humble soul and chose her to lead many souls to His Mercy" (Zaremba, 89). The novena, chaplet, and feast were also mentioned, along with some of the promises Jesus gave for those who venerated the Image of Divine Mercy.

This rather unusual broadcast concluded with the thought that Christ is warning the world that it stands on the brink of destruction, and He is inviting it to cast itself into the arms of His mercy, which desires to be the world's true Life and Happiness, Order and lasting Peace. (Zaremba, 90).

It would be many years before Faustina's name would be mentioned at the Vatican but it eventually was through Pope John Paul II. Yet, the interpretation of Christ's warning from 1948 certainly seems to have even far more relevance today than it did then.

Officially, the 20-year ban is now attributed to misunderstandings created by a faulty Italian translation of the diary, but in fact there were serious theological reservations—Faustina's claim that Jesus had promised a complete remission of sin for certain devotional acts that only the gospel can offer, for example, or what Vatican evaluators felt to be an excessive focus on Faustina herself. What is known however is that John Paul had never pushed any other devotion further or faster than this one. While it would take over thirty years for the Vatican to start talking about Faustina again, it seems to come at just the right time—when the world suddenly seems to be on the verge of destruction. Surely we all have to really ask ourselves how long can the world continue on the path we are currently on?

Certainly, nobody quite knows where our world is heading but on 17 January 2007, something happened that may provide an indication. The Bulletin of the Atomic Scientists (BAS) who have monitored how close the world is to doomsday for decades announced that it was about to move the minute hand of the Doomsday Clock two minutes closer to midnight to reflect how close we are to the end. The scientists cited global failures to solve the problems posed by nuclear weapons and the climate crisis. The decision to move the clock was not taken lightly but made following serious consultation with 18 Nobel Laureates.

The movement of the Doomsday clock certainly stands to remind us of the realities we currently face. Natural disasters, the threat of global warming, war in the Middle East, and terrorist attacks on every continent have also added fuel to our concerns. And while it would be easy to justify the writing of this book as a warning to future generations in a world where various nations are within minutes of being able to launch a nuclear holocaust, it may be time to let the world see the image the Vatican believes was Divinely imparted to Faustina.

Did 18 Nobel laureates-some of the most brilliant people in the world, move the minute hand of the 'Doomsday Clock' from seven to five minutes to midnight to simply alarm us? Or were their actions a wake up call to the world to remind us all that planet earth is spinning out of control? Did they in fact realize that we are all in need of a reminder concerning the potentially awful path we as the human race have set ourselves upon?

In the words of St. Faustina's greatest advocate, Pope John Paul II, is it conceivable that only a higher power knows what lays ahead for us and that Faustina's mission and messages are part of a Divine plan? It is interesting to reflect the late Pontiff's words at Faustina's canonization in St Peter's Square in Rome:

> *What will the years ahead bring us? What will man's future on earth be like? We are not given to know. However, it is certain that in addition to new progress there will unfortunately be no lack of painful experiences. But the light of divine mercy, which the Lord in a way wished to return to the world through Sr Faustina's charism, will illumine the way for the men and women of the third millennium.*

John Paul II's wishes can of course only be honored if the world is aware of *The Image* and the messages of *The Diary*. In reading this story, we hope his wish has been achieved and that Pope John Paul II who touched people of all faiths throughout his life may be listened to again even in death. On the back of this book you will find the Image, Christ instructed Faustina to have painted. In seeing this image, you will have played a part in Christ's plan that the whole world should have access to it. Additionally, in doing so you have helped to fulfill the last wish of Pope John Paul II, who believed it was his duty to let everyone know the messages Christ imparted to Saint Faustina, and to see the Image He told her to have painted. This was an Image which came with great hope, and should serve as a reminder that we are not alone.

"My child, life on earth is a struggle indeed: a great struggle for my kingdom, but fear not, because you are not alone. I am always supporting you. Struggle fearing nothing.

—Diary entry 1488

ENDS

We can be sure that our beloved Pope is standing today at the window of the Father's house, that sees us and blesses us. —Cardinal Ratzinger's homily at Pope John Paul II funeral Mass.

Made in the USA
Lexington, KY
22 June 2011